MY NEAR DEATH EXPERIENCE

EXPERIENCE

from A to Z

Venia R.

CONTENTS

Cover Design: Brianna Jarzyna

VENIA R

To 1 7 2, you are my life

FOREWARD

I am personally not a fan of reading the foreward section of any book, and sometimes don't. So I won't torture anyone with a long drawn out one.

I will just say that every single topic discussed in this book, came from either my Near Death Experience, my visit to the Void, or the Outer Body Experiences I've had. This book isn't about me necessarily, or my opinions, but what I've seen and learned directly, through those experiences mentioned above.

I feel it is important for those who have had some type of direct connect to the spheres of the universe, to share the knowledge gained in the most honest and least opinionated way possible. So let's jump right in...

The Spiral of Love

THE NEAR DEATH EXPERIENCE

I was 17, filled with a lust for adventure, and bursting at the seams because my parents were sending me on a school trip to Italy.

In anticipation of going overseas for the first time, I could hardly sleep leading up to the days prior to the trip, which seemed like it would never come.

What made this trip extra special for me was that my father was half Sicilian, his mother immigrated from Sicily in the early 1900's. Although we had no relationship with her, or her people - she passed when my father was very young - we felt a connection.

Finally, the day arrived, and my excitement was off the charts. In typical teenage fashion, I barely managed a goodbye wave to my parents and was off!

Nothing could spoil my joy. Not the seemingly endless plane ride, which was my first ever. Nor the extreme culture shock I experienced at arriving at such a super crowded airport, in a foreign county. The airport was filled with so many races and ethnicities I had never seen before. Some were so utterly foreign to me, they could have been from another planet, but I didn't care. To me, the whole experience was awesome!

As we all boarded a bus that was to take us to our hotel, I was positive the real adventure awaited. I had no idea how right I was. Not ten minutes into that fateful bus ride, I died, literally.

What happened was, I had been too excited to sleep on the plane. Combine that, with the days prior of missing sleep, and I was exhausted. Of course, now that we'd arrived, I figured there was no way I was going to sleep, so I would definitely need a pick me upper. Then I remembered the vitamins and caffeine pills I brought with me.

Being the typical know-it-all teen, I came up with what I thought was a brilliant idea! I had enough pills to last the entirety of the trip, so I decided to take several of the vitamins and caffeine pills in one shot. I gobbled up so many in my mouth, that a few of them spilled out. Hastily, I shoved them right back in. Yeah, I know, breathtakingly stupid. Anyway, I don't remember exactly how many I took, however, by the time we were loaded onto the bus, the caffeine was coursing through my veins with a vengeance. I felt like I could have literally crawled out of my skin. Every nerve in my body seemed to be alive and I felt a deep itch all over under my skin.

I had been partially lying down, when I started to feel my heart race. When I say race, it was beating so fast, I felt like it was going to burst from my chest at any moment.

And then strangely, I started hearing my heart race, in my bloody ears! It was so loud, it blocked out all the other sounds around me. It sounded like a train barreling down railroad tracks, picking up speed.

I wasn't sure how much more I could take of this, when after probably a minute, my heart did the opposite - it started slowing down, a lot. Frantically, I wondered was it was even possible for a heart to beat so slow? To say it was alarming would be an understatement. I let out a silent scream in pure terror.

And then my worst fear was confirmed, I couldn't hear my heart beat anymore...it had stopped. Completely. Even today, many years later, I can remember that moment vividly.

My eyes were shut at the time, so I don't know if any of my fellow classmates had been watching me, but the moment my heart stopped, my body jerked involuntarily, and my spirit just popped right out of my body.

I had not lost any consciousness, in that nano second it took to exit my body, but I felt different. One second I felt weighed down, and the next, lighter than a feather.

The terror was gone, however I had no clue what was going on. At that point, I honestly did not realize I had died, because I felt so alive, very much so.

This was weird. I was literally in two different places, two different bodies. Or was I? The me that I was looking at lying on the bus seat, appeared lifeless. This other me, that was definitely me, was alive and aware. What.the.hell?

I hovered over my body gazing down at it, stunned to see myself from that position. At that moment so much flooded my consciousness about this other me. I felt all the combined emotions of the 17 year old version of myself. It was quite overwhelming, and a wave of compassion went out to the lifeless Venia lying there.

As I gazed at my lifeless form, it occurred to me how strange I looked. I resembled a slab of meat, more than a real person. Although I weighed barely 95 pounds, from that perspective I looked more like a beached whale. And my hairstyle - yikes! In pure shallow mode, I had the audacity to wish I had styled it differently. But please cut me some slack, remember I was just 17.

Another interesting thing I noticed was the faintest of light coming from my body, compared to the bigger and more animated lights from the others on the bus. Some of the lights were solid and glowing, while others shot out as sparks of differing colors. I had never seen an auric field before, but seeing those on the bus made me realize that something wasn't right about the diminished light being emitted from my body lying there. I distinctly remember one woman in particular, who was sleeping, with her head resting on her shoulder, had more light coming from her sleeping form, than me. Her aura was reddish, mixed with sparkling lights of other darker colors. It was strange, because she was sleep, yet she obviously was feeling or dreaming about something and was feeling it intensely.

Even at this point, I still had no real idea of what was going on.

I had been facing a side window, when my attention was drawn to the huge highway we were traveling on. I decided to get a better look.

There was an Italian tour guide in the front next to the driver, speaking to us in English. I glided past them, and found myself positioned almost at the front window of the bus. It didn't hit me until afterwards, that I had literally moved through the guide. That should have been a major clue for me that I was like dead, but no, it still hadn't hit me yet. Moving through them felt slightly sticky but otherwise I hardly felt anything. I didn't have my usual sense of a body, or the space I would normally take up, so it seemed so natural to do.

I tried to grasp the metal bar at the front that went from floor to ceiling - an instinctive gesture I was used to doing when I rode public transportation to and from high school - but my hand kept sliding through it. (Another clue, duh!) Eventually I gave up that futile gesture. By the way, that metal bar, even though inanimate, had an energy field. Not quite as pronounced as the ones surrounding the actual people, but it was there nonetheless.

I hovered next to the bus driver to get a better look. I was fascinated at how fast Italians drove, and gazed in awe at the cars racing by. Part of my amazement, was that although I was a relatively new driver, I was also a fast driver, not to mention super impatient. These people were pure driving maniacs, in a good way, as far as I was concerned. I loved it!

Even more interesting, was that I could see energy flows, streaming from the cars on that highway. That really gave me a pause. Some of the energy was a light color and flowing. Other streams were dark, and chaotic. Judging by the color and patterns emitted, I could tell who was driving in a positive state of mind, and who was angry. If the energy fizzled out, it was an indication of who would be getting into an accident soon. Somehow, I instinctively knew all this. Remembering this moment many times since, has probably saved me more times than I realize in helping to keep my road rage in check.

I recall that the drivers seemed to do such an odd thing - use a turn signal to turn one way, and then speed over to the opposite direction. What I didn't realize at the time, was that I was seeing things from an omnidirectional perspective. Not only that, I was simultaneously cognizant of what was going on in the fields that paralleled the highway, and the animals that grazed along it. We passed several mountains and I was also aware that they exuded light, as well as a muted tone of some sort.

The bus company had provided two drivers, not sure why, maybe one was in training. One of the drivers mumbled a curse in

Italian at one of the cars roaring by, and my attention turned to the driver. The funny thing was I didn't hear him per se, but sensed the vibrations and emotions of him speaking. In this realm, I had different senses, like all of the five senses merged into a complete awareness of what was going on real-time: I could see, but not with eyes; I could hear, but not with ears. It sounds weird, I know.

I laser focused on the driver and my first thought was that this dude was a lunatic, and a bad tempered one at that. Almost as soon as that thought crossed my mind, a whole new view of him appeared to me, and I saw him in a different light. It was like his outer exterior was peeled away and his soul was laid bare before me.

Information about him just flooded my consciousness. I was right; the driver was short tempered, at times mean spirited, and could be unnecessarily cruel. He could also be alternately funny and grandiose when he wanted. He was a stubborn man, very sick, with numerous ailments. I saw his ailments as darker spots, that dimmed the glow coming from within him. It appeared that there was a direct correlation between his attitude and his ailments. He was miserable for so many reasons.

He had an almost unhealthy addiction to sex, which caused a few of the problems in his life. I saw that although he had a wife, he was involved with several women because of this addiction. He'd had a son with the wife, and daughters with his other women. Wew boy!

Since I have always been sensitive to others emotions, and would pick up details that most seemed oblivious to, I was not shocked at seeing some of this about this man. However, the information flooding my consciousness about him, was so much more in depth than I usually received. I could have written a book about this man.

What did shock me somewhat, was information that appeared

regarding his past lives. A trail of lifetimes this man had lived, unfolded. There was one, where he died as a young girl, no older than what I was at that time. Other than the fact of seeing him pass at a young age, that lifetime appeared unremarkable. I saw him as an African man who was very mellow and content to raise cattle. Almost the total opposite of the bellicose man before me. Then I saw him as a man who was a money collector, who was brutal when people couldn't afford to pay. One act in particular I saw, was when he scarred someone by holding a lit candle to their neck. It was then, that I noticed a dark purple colored birth mark, in the same spot on his neck here. I sensed that was no coincidence.

That was my first time really understanding that this lifetime was one of many we experience. I'd heard about reincarnation before; however, this experience really cemented my understanding, and it became more than just a theory, but was now a reality.

This knowledge had unfolded to me as naturally as a waterfall. There was nothing I couldn't know about him if I wanted to. However, there was no judgement behind what I saw. Nor was it an invasion of privacy, but more of an unfolding of the truth. In other words, I was in a realm of pure understanding and knowingness.

Soon, I sensed a presence energetically touch my soul. As soon as it did, the bus driver, highway and my lifeless body faded, and I found myself in a place of unbelievable whiteness. There was an eternal glow that was being sourced from within every particle of this white space.

It wasn't a room, but a realm. In this realm, there was a stillness. In this stillness was supreme peace and the most harmonious presence of love imaginable. My being automatically expanded in this realm. There was a sense of oneness to everything, and my spirit was connected to this oneness. I was a part of everything. I felt no separation or aloneness. I felt connected to everything that ever was. I was completely merged with this realm, yet my individuality was still intact.

I was bathed in pure love, serenity, and supreme happiness. In this realm, there was no negativity, sadness nor fear. I couldn't think a negative thought if I tried. There was nothing religious about this feeling, but I will call it divine. It was supreme love stripped of any human attributes.

I was completely energized in this realm and yet oddly super calm. As a side note: experiencing this realm is one of the main reasons drugs never held an allure for me, since I know that nothing on earth can never replicate that sublime feeling I experienced. Some drugs may come close, but I am positive they will never be able to duplicate it. To me, it would be a cheap counterfeit.

The realm was what I can only describe as ultra real. To explain, this human reality is a dimmed down version of that reality I experienced. Looking back on it now, I can see how a veil is in place when we are in human form because neither our human bodies nor brains are equipped to handle the realm of the spiritual world which contains all densities and dimensions.

We are only in the 3rd dimension here. Some may be aware of or experience slivers of the 4th dimension, but that's about it. When that veil is lifted you are free from the dimensional confinement. That not only includes your thoughts and emotions, but physique as well.

At 17, I didn't have aches or pains per se, but I did have some of the discomforts of a human body. With this spiritual body/ consciousness, I didn't experience any of those discomforts. I almost didn't feel like I had a body, but I did. It was like a loosely outlined human body, but see thru. I will call it my ethereal form. This form was outlined with a golden glow. There were points throughout my ethereal body that glowed and pulsed, and I understood them to be connection points to my physical body, astral form, higher self and soul.

In this realm, I experienced no space or distance. I knew that I could literally will myself to be anywhere. It took nothing but a mere thought, and I was there. I didn't necessarily feel like going anywhere, as I was supremely content, yet I sensed/saw so many different realities in this realm. The best way I can describe it is as if all space had collapsed onto itself so you could be anywhere at once. When you are looking out from one dimension, like our 3D world, you can only see 3D things. However, when you aren't confined to one dimension, you can travel to the others with no barriers. That's how it felt like.

My ethereal form soaked in everything. I could not get enough and there seemed to be no end to it. Fortunately, the presence that was with me, had an infinite amount of patience, as I soaked in this sublime realm.

I felt a freedom that was mentally liberating. I didn't have a care in the world. I had zero stresses. I no longer thought of my lifeless body on the bus. Not even the fact that I was in Italy. My entire being was being treated to what I can only describe as a cleansing soul massage, and I was no longer concerned with any earthly stuff. Nothing earthly mattered in this state of mind. Not that I wasn't aware of my life and family, however, I instinctively understood that where I was at was truly my home, and the other 'me' was just a part of a reality that was temporary and not the real me. As a matter of fact, I was so much more than that 17-year-old on the bus. I was a complete, loving, confident being who had lived many lives, as different species, yet I was even more than the summation of all those. My soul was a spark of the Source of everything and within me contained everything. The 17-year-old was just a small slice of a super big pie and a temporary one, because I had been around for eons. I was old as dirt.

I could literally do anything. Be a part of everything, or not. I could, in this state of being, be anything I wanted. The deepest part of me strove towards all that was good and embraced it.

In that moment of understanding, confidence was cemented into my being. I no longer felt lesser than others over some shallow comparisons. The inferiority complex I had suffered through for most of my young life, was now a fading memory.

Another thing that I connected with was love on a level that I had never felt during my 17 years, not even my mother's love. This love was healing, beautiful, unconditional, soothing, and so much more. It seeped into every nook and cranny of my being and cleansed so much from me.

It dawned on me that this was heaven. Heaven wasn't a locality, it was the realm of the spiritual world. This was home to me in the deepest sense of the word. I belonged here. But it wasn't just my home. I was subliminally aware of others in this realm, but was not intruded upon or bothered by them. Although I felt no space or separation, there seemed to be more than enough room for the many I sensed were there, with no feelings of crowding or encroachment. There were so many different types of spiritual beings, and not all were human either. I was fascinated seeing the different forms that resided in this realm, as well as the formless ones. Some had no distinctive spiritual form, but their presence was unmistakeable because we were relating consciousness to consciousness.

Within this sublime realm, were streams of sparkling light that I became aware of. Within these strobes of light, were parts of heaven that branched onto other creations of the heavenly worlds. It seemed like these went on forever and branched out into more and more rarified worlds. I knew somehow, that not all were privy to some of those worlds. They were so divine, that I knew in my current form as well as state of my spirit, I was not privy to those worlds. My soul, the highest essence of myself, could tap into those realms because the soul is pure and the direct spark of that divine. But the Venia that was experiencing this realm, could not partake of those more advanced ones.

However, I did not feel shortchanged or rejected knowing this, because what I was experiencing was so deeply satisfying and perfect, for me. My true home.

The infinite levels of creation were so beautiful and multifaceted. I could imagine anything and it was a reality there. And yet it didn't feel like imagination, but just an extension of me in creative form. In spiritual form I was pure consciousness, yet could have a form or body that was suited to my unique vibrations. I was able to create a reality of whatever was familiar to me. All this I surmised while experiencing the multi faceted realm of this spiritual zone.

After what seemed like an eternity, the presence with me gently nudged by mind by a form of complete thought transference. There was no auditory speaking between us, but thoughts, images, feelings, emotions and understanding were impressed upon me and received all at once. Through this complete process of communication, they revealed to me that they were my guide. I asked what a guide was, and was told I would understand soon enough. (I describe my guide in the chapter *Spirit Guides*)

I didn't feel intruded upon by this entity claiming to be my guide. Instead, I felt they were acting from a place of deep love and concern for me, and I felt no impulse to resist. I sensed that we shared a deep connection, more so than my immediate family members, yet somehow I couldn't place it. I now know, that the veil of secrecy was there on purpose, because an explanation of our bond would no doubt have influenced me. And I sensed no pressure from this entity, to force me into anything. Fortunately for me, I went with my instincts, and willingly accepted this being, my guide.

There was now an understanding of trust between us. My guide did reveal that we had agreed to meet like this before I entered earth as Venia. There were reasons for it that would eventually unfold in the short and long term.

For now though, I was told we were going to travel.

At my consent, the white realm faded, and a portal seemed to peel open from out of nowhere...

And I experienced what to me was the adventure of a lifetime. An experience I can never forget, nor do I want to. And I've put most of it in this book.

It took me years to mentally unpack the whole experience. I had had a near death experience, but did not realize it at the time, as this was not a common topic back then. As a matter of fact, I don't recall hearing anyone talk about it.

At 17, I did not have the life experience nor maturity to appreciate its value. I allowed this experience to lie dormant in me for years, while I kept trying to process it, telling no one. Not even close family.

In between trying to live my life as a young adult, serving in the military and then becoming a mother and wife, I would relive the experience over and over mentally. All the while I kept it inside, nurturing it. The amazing thing was that instead of diminishing my memory, time seemed to preserve it, and reveal even more details.

It wasn't until reading Betty J. Eadie's book, <u>Embraced by the Light</u>, about her Near Death Experience, did I start to truly appreciate and understand what I'd experienced. Although our NDE's were vastly different, with few similarities, I could relate to her NDE, and for the first time I had some sort of framework to go by. Eventually, the pieces of the puzzle started coming together, bit by bit. The knowledge I'd learned helped me tremendously during certain periods of my life.

Years later, I wrote a book and tried to incorporate some of what I saw in my experience, but I was not ready, nor prepared to discuss my NDE openly, and the book reflected my reluctance.

Now, things have changed. Two things prompted me to write

this book. The first involves two people I love dearly, my Aunt Joyce and soul sister Rhonda. Unbeknownst to each other, they started rereading my previous book at about the same time, and as a result urged me to write another. I have no doubt they were being encouraged from the other side. They were not aware of the details of my NDE, no one was, however I took this as a clear sign that it was time to reveal it and the other experiences I've had.

Second, I am no longer hesitant about sharing my experience. I had what I call a vision, which I believe was my guide nicely but firmly bullying me, where I was shown I had completed my second book. Even down to the image I was to use on the cover. When the spirit world prompts you, it is best not to ignore it, as I have learned. So, other than a few extremely personal details, I'm not holding back, nor do I care to. I am no longer concerned if it sounds insane, crazy, far-fetched or if anyone believes me. I am aware that some of it reads like a fantasy novel, and that's ok. If the spirit world gives something its approval, you can best believe, it is the right thing to do.

I take my willingness to write this book now, so many years later, as a sign of what my guide spoke about when they told me that the reasons would unfold in the long term for my having the NDE.

I am confident this book will resonate with some. It's the truth of what I experienced, and it may not be anyone else's truth and that is completely fine. If nothing else, my aim is that it helps you find your truth and makes some sense out of this existence while you are here. I learned that there is no ultimate truth for everyone, we all have our own unique agenda on why we came here. Each of us must travel our own path in this life, and no two will be the same because we each came here to learn different things, unique to our soul's journey.

As you read further you will understand why I could not fabricate anything in this book, because I am not willing to risk my soul integrity to do so. Nothing is more important to me than that.

Since having the NDE, I've had several out of body experiences which are quite different from my NDE. The outer body experiences (OBE's) I've had were when my consciousness was propelled from this third-dimension realm, into the spiritual zone of reality. I had no guide, nor did I do anything consciously to trigger them, i.e, I hadn't been meditating or taking drugs. They happened spontaneously. I believe those experiences were the result of me having the NDE initially and dipping into that other realm. I will also incorporate what I saw during these OBEs in this book.

I've got to warn you, some of this information is very unconventional and may challenge some long held beliefs. It is up to reader to decide what to do with the information.

I have written this book in topic format and in each subject, I will share parts of those journeys. The topics are laid out alphabetically, to make them easier to locate. To me it is the best way I can relay the multi-faceted things I was shown.

The book was purposely written so you do not have to read it sequentially; you can browse through, or read it from cover to cover at your leisure.

Welcome to my journey!

ABORTION

Let me start this chapter off by saying that I have had an abortion, and I feel that it is important to note that it was after my NDE.

During my NDE the process of birth (see chapter titled *Incarnating*), was revealed to me. What always begins the process, is a soul deciding it wants to incarnate for whatever reason; be it to work on karma, help loved ones with theirs, experience life in human form, or a myriad of individual reasons. The soul does not actually incarnate, it is the spiritual form of that soul, that will reside in a human body.

According to my guide, when a pregnancy occurs, it is an opportunity in the spirit world for those souls who have decided to incarnate. A spirit is assigned to that future birth by numerous factors. Once the decision is made on which spirit will occupy the fetus, they will begin planning their life ahead. So many details of the persons life are orchestrated from the other side, and it is a complex process in which the incoming soul is an integral part of.

The spirit that is to incarnate, will typically not enter the fetus until right up to the moment before birth. It is extremely rare for a spirit to enter the fetus before that time; as stated above, because it is too busy planning its life ahead. The spirit does not reside in the fetus at this point.

There are exceptions, as some choose to experience a brief time inside the womb, but most enter either right before birth or the first breath, and sometimes even after.

I was shown by my guide, that I personally entered my mother's womb the week prior to my birth, four days before, to be exact. I chose to experience the cramped feeling of being inside the womb for a few days, and that up until the actual day of birth, I withdrew a few times, traveling back and forth between the two worlds. The fact that spirits could go back and forth during this period, I found fascinating. My guide explained that it was quite normal, since the spirit had not made the connection to the human brain yet, and was not tethered in place. It could literally travel at will.

When a soul chooses the vessel (mother) it is to be born to, it is always free to withdraw itself from that future birth if conditions in the mother's life change, to the point where that life will no longer serve that soul as planned. When this happens, its usually what we refer to as a still birth or SIDs.

A miscarriage occurs when the spirit assigned to the fetus, decides not to incarnate. The spirit is never damaged in that process. To put it simply, the spirit has changed its' mind and decided not to incarnate, or it will find another vessel (mother) to be born to.

As for the pregnancy that resulted in my son's birth, I was initially pregnant with twins. My son's fraternal twin elected not to be born, resulting in my having a partial miscarriage during my 5th month. Fortunately, my son survived and thrived in the womb, and was eventually born perfectly healthy. I believe from what I've seen and felt, that the twin that chose to vacate my pregnancy, came back through my son as his child, one of my grandchildren.

There are also other reasons the spirit may vacate the assignment of a fetus at this point, that have more to do with the parents and their learning, and/or karma.

In the case of abortion, I was shown that **no spirit will be assigned to a fetus that is to be aborted**. Period. It is literally that cut and dry, when viewed from the other side. There is absolutely no stigma attached to it, and it definitely was not looked upon as a so-called sin or murder. Souls are in no way effected by abortion, and can never be destroyed, by any means. Knowing this, it saddens me how it has caused all sorts of division, controversy and even violence here.

In my own life, my reason for having an abortion was that I felt deep down that I was not ready to have a child, at that specific period of time. The thought of being a mother, filled me with dread. I understood from my NDE that no soul would be sacrificed in my decision so I didn't need to carry any guilt regarding my decision.

The wisdom and forethought displayed by guide - since at the time of my NDE I was not even having sexual relations - is indicative of a scene I was shown way back then, that I believe is so pertinent today. I was showed an abortion clinic with people standing outside, yelling and taunting those who were trying to gain access and have the procedure. There was snow on the ground, and people were sliding as they hastily tried to make their way inside. Those who were trying to enter, were already anxious about having an abortion, and the people who were harassing them, weren't helping. After it was understood that I fully comprehended the scene I was being shown, my guide simply asked me, 'who do you think is incurring karma here?' I didn't need to answer my guide, because I knew it was a rhetorical question. The ones who displayed the anger, were the ones incurring karma. Although they felt they were righteous in their anger, they were sadly mistaken. They had no right to judge or spew hate.

I don't believe anyone ever thinks - Yay, today I am going to have an abortion! In fact, it's often a very life changing somber decision, that is typically not made lightly. It certainly wasn't in my case. However, because of what I understood from my NDE, as I stated in the beginning of this chapter, I did not put myself through unnecessary guilt or anxiety. As my guide lovingly showed me, those emotions were not necessary, nor should they be a part of the decision regarding having an abortion.

ADVENTURE OUT
IN SPACE

As a teen, I used to gaze up at the stars from my bedroom window. I could see the constellations and stars, and my imagination was fueled, trying to envision what lie out there in that vast black wonderland. I was pretty certain that other life forms existed on other planets, that huge space couldn't be just for humans. I also knew that space was bigger than even I could imagine, although I truly had no idea how big it was. That was about as close as I came to the truth, until I had an out of body experience, which shook me to my core.

It happened after I laid down one night, and couldn't fall asleep. I was so deeply relaxed however, that my astral form slipped out of my body, zoomed out of my bed, through my bedroom ceiling and shot straight up into space. It took mere seconds to figure out that I was past the earth's orbit, and out into the velvety blackness of space. I remember seeing a shimmering grey malleable cord from my body in bed, connected to myself out in space, swaying slightly. I had no idea what it was but wasn't too focused on it because of where I'd landed.

I will never forget the mind-numbing feeling of space, surrounding me. There was a palpable blackness interspersed with pinpoints of lights from objects unbelievably and unimaginably far away. Space was so expansive, so massive that I was overwhelmed. If I stayed any longer, I felt it would also blow my mind, literally. I could no longer take it, and willed myself back into my safe environment, my body in bed. My curiosity was squelched for the moment, and I didnt desire or seek a repeat of that experience. In other words, I majorly punked out.

Fast forward years later...

During my NDE, after I had spent some time in the beautiful white realm, my guide (see chapter titled *Spirit Guides*) indicated we were going to travel. I wasn't told the destination, and I didn't get a read from my guide where we'd be travelling to, but I was game. Little did I know the adventure awaiting me.

A portal opened and my ethereal form was gathered into my guide's orb, which expanded to accommodate me. My guide's orb was a beautiful soft yellowish white. I became an orb of light also. Mind you, I did nothing to make that transformation happen, it was orchestrated somehow by my guide. Since I did not have a physical body, I did not feel a physical change. But I did feel a merging of energy with my guide. The best way I can describe it is the embracing feeling you get when stepping into a bath tub full of warm water.

We traveled through a lighted tunnel of swirling energy, that somehow was also controlled by my guide. Traveling this way felt instaneous. One moment we were in the white realm, and the next we were out in space.

Whoa! Space was vast, mind numbingly so, as I previously saw. However, let me say that there are really no words to describe how massive it is. No matter from which direction I gazed, there seemed to be no end. It was overwhelming, even within the protection of my guide's orb. And to think, as vast as space is, it is a physical phenom and yet the spiritual world is even so much more. So that should give you a clue about how utterly mind blowing, fantastic and awesome the spiritual realm is.

Since we were in spiritual form, I was seeing space from an entirely different perspective. This time I could see details about it that I hadn't noticed previously during my brief astral trip. Space was alive. Even the parts that appeared empty or completely black, were filled with an energy of some sort that I cannot describe, because it has no earthly equivalent that I know of. I truly feel sorry for those reading this because I am not a scientist, and thus I cannot even begin to translate what I saw into scientific jargon. But I will do my best.

I saw that there was a fabric to space, that contained energy. This fabric was invisible to the naked eye, yet existed nonetheless. Currents of this energy, filled every nook and cranny. These currents were broken down into geometric-type flows. There were elements to these currents, smaller than the smallest element we know of. These elements weren't made up of the density of matter. They were something else, a part of an invisible network of existence that is always present. I could see its form perpetuating itself endlessly. It was amazing. I was dazzled by these particles, that were operating from some type of intelligent source, and could have observed them forever.

It was about this time, when I became aware of the faint sound of musical chords. Not song, but tones. These tones were soft, yet unmistakeable. They seemed to be present throughout. The tones were harmonious, perfect and sounded heavenly. There seemed to be no source of them, yet they were omnipresent.

I was focused on the fabric of space and the beautiful music of the spheres, when my guide pointed out several traveling spacecraft. Since I was able to focus on more than one thing, due to being outside the confines and limitations of my human brain, I was able to simultaneously process the myriad of things going on.

Some of these spacecraft were travelling so fast, they appeared as streaks of light, barely discernable as objects. I've seen shooting stars and can tell the difference. These craft, also moved faster than the movement of those dying stars, and with purpose. They were intelligently operated craft. Some of the craft changed density mid flight. In other words they were visible one way, and then moments later transformed themselves into another shape entirely. Some appeared and disappeared, as if they were phasing in and out of dimensions.

Other craft appeared stationary, like huge floating cities. One in particular was so massive, that I mistook it for a planet. My guide corrected me, showing me a zoomed in version, where I could see it was actually made of some type of metallic substance, that was almost a burnished copper color. Although at first glance I thought the ship was stationary, I noticed that it was ever so slowly spinning. My guide informed me that the inhabitants of that ship were travellers from far, far away. Their entire civilization resided on that ship and they were roamers, who called no planet home. The beings were able to traverse the universe at will. I was also told that they weren't humanoid type beings, and I would probably be petrified if I saw them. I took that at face value and did not inquire further.

I understood from what my guide showed me, that the alien species we saw, knew how to manipulate the energy that flowed throughout space. Their craft harnessed the energy patterns and flows while travelling or stationary. The energy was powerful and did not break down. It was self-generating.

There were two items that my guide impressed upon me at that time regarding space travel, that I have no idea what they mean, but I will freely share them:

TE

$$A=RU^2$$

I have never tried to figure out their meaning, however before I am criticized for this, remember I had a first hand view of space that even those who manage to figure out those cryptic formulas, or whatever they are, will still not be able to duplicate what I witnessed. Also, as I explained earlier, I do not have a scientific bent to my mind, and am not particularly interested in figuring out what they mean. Call me lazy, but the reality is that once back in my true spiritual form, I will be able to traverse space at will.

My guide was showing me so much, and this time I was no punk, I was hungry for more. Space was literally teeming with life. I recognized souls, like me, traveling through space. There were orbs everywhere, darting here and there, about their business. They, like me, were traveling without the aid of a ship. The orbs were all different colors and shapes. The ones traveling extremely fast had orbs that appeared to be flattened. Others were traveling as if they were tourists taking in the sights. I wondered, were their bodies, like mine, back on earth? Were they from other planets? Were they inhabitants of the spirit world? Whatever the case may be, it was fascinating. I felt a kinship with them as they traveled. And I realized that no one on earth would believe people traveled this way.

I learned that there were layers, upon layers of dimensional travel that existed, that we could not see from earth. There was more traffic in space than our busiest highways on earth combined, yet there was no congestion or crowding. Besides the planets visible to us, there were many more that were not. Meaning there were many interstellar systems, that were on a different spectrum than the third dimension. These systems were layered upon each other, yet amazingly did not effect each other.

My guide showed me several planets in our own solar system, that we were not even aware of. I asked why we couldn't see them from earth, since they were so visible to me in this realm, and appeared so close. It was explained, that they fluctuated between density's (not dimensions, apparently there is a difference) and are not visible to the spectrum of the human eye or its instruments, although eventually we would evolve to the point where we were able to pick up a hint of movements from some of these planets.

There were also many life forms that inhabited space, that were not planets or celestial bodies. Creatures that I have no idea how to categorize. One in particular, seemed to be a moving nebula. It looked like a typical interstellar cloud, yet behaved and moved with purpose, self-guidance and intelligence. And then it condensed and expanded itself into an almost loosely outlined human type form at will, and seemed to be able to travel great distances. That was extremely weird seeing this humungous humanoid out in space. I know how unbelievable that sounds, yet I saw it.

Another life form I saw, was a prehistoric looking creature that took up residence on an asteroid. The creature was huge, greyish in color and resembled a tardigrade in almost every way, except it didn't have as many legs, and its size; the tardigrade is a microscopic critter, whereas the creature I saw was easily the size of a four or five story building. It is interesting to note the tardigrade can withstand any type of extreme conditions, including nuclear radiation. So, seeing a similar creature out in space, was not unimaginable.

Next, we traveled just a bit, I believe it was incredibly far, yet, it didn't seem to take us long. The same method of travel was used; being condensed into a portal/tunnel, and then expanding back to our orb spheres.

Within moments we had arrived at my guides' destination.

The planetary system we'd arrived at, my guide explained, was not in earths solar system, but in our galaxy. I was curious about this, but had no real knowledge of Astronomy, and thus could not grasp a sense of its location. Besides there didn't seem to be any north, south, east, or west as a gauge for me to go by. My guide sensed my lack of understanding, and offered an explanation in layman's terms; that if you projected all the way out in space from Australia, during their nighttime, in their summertime season, you would eventually reach it. Hmm. Still didn't quite help, but ok.

We didn't arrive at a planet, but a massive structure that hung in space. Given its size, it could have been a small planet like the one we had just seen, yet this structure wasn't spherical like a planet. Its shape was constantly changing. The best way I can describe it; is if the pieces of a lego kit were haphazardly put together and constantly rearranging themselves.

The structure appeared to be made up of some type of bio crystalline type substance. Its shape grew and expanded as needed, into whatever shape was necessary to hold its inhabitants. I knew that it did not operate with the same laws of physics we had on earth.

This ship/structure was teeming with organic crystalline beings. The beings could merge into the structures, created by them, and manipulate them as needed. Kaleidoscope type lights glistened off these beings and their surroundings.

I knew these beings couldn't be seen by humans, because they appeared almost invisible to me in this realm. I only caught their shape when they were in motion, by a very thin outline, that gave them away. Nonetheless, they were very much real and solid.

I was told they were a warrior type of race, but not violently so. More like they provided some type of security to others, in their same section of space.

They were a humanoid race, with two arms and two legs. Their head was in the shape of a human head, but that is where the comparison ends. There was no nose and no mouth. There were two eyes that were the same crystalline material as their bodies, but they were like slits. The eyes widened and shut vertically. The eyes covered most of what you could call their face, giving their face the appearance of all eyes. They did have ears but they were tiny, like the size of a quarter and similar to their eyes. Their skin was a shiny type material, with a silver hue, when they weren't merged with their structures.

It was quite difficult to distinguish between these beings. There didn't appear to be any discernable sex that I could identify, and to my eye, they all looked alike.

There was also no way to gauge how many of these beings existed because some of them were seamlessly merged into the buildings. At times, it was impossible to differentiate between one of their buildings, and an actual being.

I've got to be honest, these creatures were super foreign to me. Not to mention, they did not look or act anything like humans. They didn't appear to be robotic, yet at the same time they didn't appear to display any emotions. I could not draw any parallels with them, in regards to a living being.

At 17, this was a bit much for me to handle, and honestly, I was quite dismissive of them. I was almost rude, as rude as one can be as a spiritual being. But a face with just eyes!? Naw! I couldn't do it.

My guide sensed my indifference (ignorance), but seemed nonplussed. Instead, they indicated we were leaving this section of space and traveling to another world, that was in the same galaxy, but vastly different than the one we'd just witnessed.

Now of course, I am filled with deep regret regarding my lack of curiosity, and the fact that I didn't request more information from my guide. What was I thinking!?

We arrived at an actual planet this time.

Woa! My guide wasn't kidding! This world was not only different than the one we'd just came from, but vastly different from earth.

Right away I could see that this planet had three moons, orbiting around a very light blue sun. To say that this was odd, would be an understatement. From my perspective, I had only ever seen our sun, and suns were supposed to be yellow. To see this pale blue shining sun was definitely a shocker.

The planets moons' colors were a sort of beige, red and green and they seemed oddly close together. From where we hovered, I could tell they were extremely close to the planet. In perspective, its moons appeared much closer to this planet, than our moon was to earth.

The sky was not blue, however, but sort of the beige color of one of the moons. And it seemed as if there were clouds everywhere, but they weren't all white. More like a mixture of beige, tinted with blue.

This planet was also mostly made up of water. There were small islands scattered here and there, but no huge land masses. The water appeared clear, but with a blueish tint, no doubt due to its sun. You could see storms constantly rolling across the great expanse of its waters.

Initially, I didn't see any life on the surface, and I questioned my guide. I was told that this world consisted strictly of marine inhabitants. Not only that, but it was one of the original marine worlds inhabited eons ago, and that some of earths marine inhabitants were transplants from there. I was told this was the reason for the visit to this particular planet. To be told that creatures from other planets were purposely transplanted to earth was quite a concept. I filed that into the definitely think about this later category.

Eventually, I started to see evidence of life. Marine animals were darting from the oceans. One creature that resembled a brontosaurus, in the sense that it had an elongated neck and huge lower body, rose from the water, flew a bit flapping its appendages, then dove back into the water. It appeared too large to fly as far as I was concerned, yet there it was, like a huge elephant in the sky.

There was one dolphin type creature who captured my eye. It had the shape of a dolphin, but was much bigger than ours, and white, not grey. It seemed to be putting on a show. It would rise out of the water, twirl around and then dive back in. It did this many times in several different ways - front flips, back flips and even partially suspending itself in the air while doing it. The dolphin displayed a remarkable intelligence, that was astonishing. It was later joined by several other dolphins, who performed these same acrobatic feats in perfect sync. How they did this was fascinating, as they moved as one. This encounter is where I get my love for these fascinating creatures.

My guide eventually took us underwater. Since I did not have a physical body I did not feel the human effects when water touches a body, however I felt just as free and alive below the surface as I did above it. We moved easily and swiftly. It was an exhilarating feeling.

I have to say that our best CGI could never replicate what I saw below. I recently saw the film Aqua Man, and although it did come close, it did not duplicate the wonders I saw. Also, unlike the film, I did not see humans underwater, however there were humanoid aquatic life forms, what we would call mermaids, and there were many varieties of them. I had to process this. It was truly shocking to see these creatures that I had only heard about in fairy tales. And not only that but they came in many different varieties and colors; green, blue, pink, brown and even albino ones.

Some had fins, with webbed hands, and what we know as a mermaid tail. Others had humanoid type arms, which were very muscled, along with several leg appendages, almost like an octopus. There were some I saw whose legs were melded together, with no tail, and a powerful upper body. Some of these aquatic beings had scaley type skin, with spindly protrusions down their backs. The albino version had no scales, and their skin was very smooth. Some had gills on their faces, while others had them running down their backs. They all maneuvered the water skillfully, no matter the body type.

When we first traveled underwater my guide and I were mere observers of this world. Then my guide widened its' orb and we suddenly became visible to these creatures. I don't know if it was done on my behalf, but I was grateful, to an extent. Ok, side note here: some of these creatures would have scared the life out of me, if I had not been surrounded within the protective cloak of my guide. When I say they were humanoid, I mean their physiques were similar to humans, however that is where the comparison ends. They had feral facial characteristics: some had blood red or yellow slits for eyes - granted their eyes were probably designed that way as a result of living under water - but it sure didn't help to soften their looks; all of them appeared to have huge pointed teeth, like sharks; others had muscles in their faces, that contracted with each breath. By their size alone, they looked like they could crush a human, with very little effort, if provoked. And although they didn't act hostile, their temperament didn't appear all that sweet.

As a result of my guide making us visible, several of the creatures swam towards us, stopping a safe distance away, but making it known they could see us. They did not appear scared or frightened, but curious, as I was of them. Their actions were swift and powerful, not quite hostile, but guarded, as they swam in our periphery.

I was not able to communicate with them but understood their actions; I was as foreign to them as they were to me. I could tell they sensed no hostility from us either, and they became increasingly, albeit cautiously friendly, darting closer and closer to us.

My guide and I had an audience that included several of the different species of these mer creatures, as well as non-human types of marine animals. I could see them communicating with each other regarding us and there appeared to be total understanding amongst all the species. The various methods of communication, which I explain below, was reflected in tiny strobes of electric lights that shot out and lit up the underbelly of the planet's ocean. Judging by the number of lights that could be seen, there was plenty going on. There even appeared to be communication with the whales, some of which appeared much larger than the size of our largest; the blue whale.

There was an abundance of foliage underwater. Some of it appeared to be just a vegetative food source, while some appeared as intelligent and sentient as the beings that inhabited the waters.

I saw huge structures underneath the water that were bioluminescent. They were beautiful aesthetically, and glowed with a life of their own. There was a beautiful bluish glow coming from some of these structures/buildings that was oddly the exact shade of their sun. I somehow knew/sensed this was done purposely. There were no hard outlines to the structures, they had a smooth flow to their design. I wondered how they were built, especially being underwater, but I didn't wonder for long.

Our audience grew measurably. The creatures surrounding us were not trying to communicate with me or my guide directly, but appeared as if they were gossiping about us. Somehow, word spread, and more and more creatures gathered. I saw creatures with fish bodies and humanoid heads. There were some that resembled the manatees of Florida, that displayed an almost human like intelligence, and when at rest they stood upright on their powerful tails. I have to admit, that at the time of seeing those creatures, I had never seen nor heard of a manatee. It wasn't until years later, while stationed in Florida, that I first saw one. I literally dropped to my knees, stunned at seeing one on earth. This was additional confirmation for me personally of my NDE.

Several of the underwater creatures I saw literally had no heads, just appendages, yet appeared sentient. There were creatures we know as Seahorses that were bigger than the size of a car. They were so huge, I didn't realize at first, they were larger versions of the seahorses we have here. I could go on and on about the numerous creatures that inhabited those waters.

My guide did not seem alarmed at our growing audience, thankfully! As a matter of fact, my guide seemed to be able to communicate with them, darn near all of them. There was quite a bit of back and forth between them and my guide. Communication was not linear in the human sense, nor was any of it spoken. It seemed as if the mer creatures and other beings were all communicating at once with my guide in the mix.

One of the methods of communication seemed to be pulses of electricity. The pulses, depending on the messages being sent out, varied in intensity. Another appeared to be the creation of bubbles. Several of the marine animals could project millions of bubbles that formed undercurrent waves. Other species emitted clicks and sonar waves. The mer people seemed to have several methods of communication; it seemed like they were able to mimic almost every form of communication used by all of the species.

At one point my guide shot out a huge bolt of brilliant light towards one of the mer people. I believe this was the being whom you could call their leader, however I am not positive about that.

It was not a hostile act, and apparently received quite well, because to my surprise they responded with an almost equally brilliant electric pulse of light, although not as big as my guides. Somehow, I understood it to be a sign of respect, and they were saying goodbye. All in one. Fascinating!

Noting my fascination, my guide explained to me that there was a universal language, and that if you tap into it you can communicate with all creatures at their level of understanding. My guide then projected the understanding of that universal language to me. It is made of up symbols and energy patterns associated with those symbols. Thus the transference of the bolt of light energy. I was also told, that that this world was just a very small sample of the worlds that existed.

Ok, cool! I could relate to this world, and was not eager to leave but it seemed like we were. I asked if we could visit more worlds. My guide gently, but firmly negated my request, explaining that when I was back in spirit form, I could visit anywhere I like. I was told that I have already traveled to many worlds, I just did not remember them, but I would once I was back in my true form. Jokingly, my guide teased that when I did travel in my spirit form, I should definitely come back to this world, since it appeared I had many fans.

It was time to go and my guide whisked us back to the white realm. Its worth noting that my guide opened up the portal while we were still in the ocean, and we traveled from there.

Once back in the white realm, we were gently separated and I was back to my ethereal form.

I marveled at what I had just experienced, and knew that I would never forget it. With all that I just saw, it made me think of all that I was never told. And the denials. Back when I was a teenager, the government was in the habit of firmly denying the existence of extraterrestrials. Now, it seemed ridiculous, absurdly so. And I needed to know the truth.

I asked my guide about aliens visiting earth. My guide responded that not only do they visit earth, but some were living among us, and had bases on our planet. And that I would be shocked at how many there were, and the traffic that earth received from other-worldly beings.

Although my guide didn't elaborate, I was told that earth was actually owned and run by other-worldly beings. There was a finality to what was said that did not warrant any further query, so I did not question anymore.

Since I have witnessed first hand life on other planets and worlds, there is not a soul on this earth or beyond that can convince me that alien life does not exist. I know what I saw and experienced. To me it is the height of supreme arrogance to assume that amidst a universe filled with so many stars and galaxies, we are the only life among them.

Many of us have been to other planets as different species and feel it deep down. I have often heard people say that earth feels foreign to them. Like they don't feel like they belong here. And for some, that may be true. Earth may not be their true home, and they are homesick for another world.

AGENDA

Near the end of my NDE, the very last thing I asked my guide was how should I live (see chapter titled *How it all ended*). After all that I had just experienced, my 17 year old mind was propelled into a deeper mindset, and at that moment, I was unsure of how to live my life, and more importantly, what was my purpose in life? I loved ballet and had often dreamt of myself becoming a famous ballerina. Yet deep down, I knew that I hadn't put in the work nor did I have the true desire to pursue that particular rigorous profession.

Since I was an open book, as far as my guide was concerned, they agreed with me that becoming a ballerina was not my path this time around. Fortunately, my guide was able to sense/see the real meaning behind my question and answered me accordingly. My guide explained that we all come here on this earth with a soul agenda. We came here with a plan, whether it was; to challenge ourselves, to grow, to experience, accomplish, work through karma, or to simply enjoy life.

I was told that all soul agendas are unique, and no two are alike, not even identical twins. Thus, we cannot judge another or compare ourselves to another, because we are here to experience things others may not. And vice versa. We are not equipped with the same life experiences, circumstances, and character traits.

My guide probably read my mind, when they pointed out that not everyone is destined to be rich or famous. A person may have achieved those things in another lifetime, or, it is just not part of their souls' focus. People may come here to work on certain qualities like kindness, or a positive attitude towards life, and material gains are not important to them.

Personally, I know that patience is one of the things I have come here to work on. I was born with none. I have always wanted everything immediately, if not yesterday. The good thing about not having patience is I am not a procrastinator; if something needs to be done, I rarely delay or put it aside for later. On the flip side though, my impatience has caused others to feel uneasy around me, and created some tense situations where I've unnecessarily rushed things. So naturally, the universe has thrown plenty of situations my way, where I am forced to be patient. Like, I almost always find myself behind the slowest driver on the road, whom I'm unable to pass. I typically seem to hit every red light when driving. Or, when waiting in line, as soon as it's my turn a problem arises - like the cash register runs out of paper or a shift change. And since I am too impatient to ever read instructions, I usually put things together wrong, and end up having to read the instructions anyway. I am definitely a work in progress.

I was a little shocked to hear from my guide, that some people come to simply enjoy life. They don't experience the heartaches or hardships that others seem to. To them, life is one big party. We all know someone like this, and have probably passed judgement upon them as being shallow. However they are probably fulfilling their agenda, it just may not vibe with our preplanned idea of how life should be to work hard, and take everything seriously. These people may have earned a vaca life of sorts; the right to just enjoy life, after fulfilling some demanding karmic obligations in previous lives. We just can't see the bigger picture while here on earth.

There are some people whom we can see right away were born with a specific agenda, they slide right into their roles with perfection. To me, President Zelensky of Ukraine is one of those people. Richard Pryor's soul agenda was obvious; he came to make us laugh. John Lennon came to deliver a message through song. Martin Luther Kings' agenda was to elevate the black race to themselves and others. Another person with a clear agenda was my late maternal grandmother. She raised 10 children, all while working full time as a nurses' aide, whereas I struggled trying to raise one child, working full time. She was a natural.

There are other's we meet who don't seem to have a clear agenda or theirs isn't as obvious. Yet they fulfill their agenda working behind the scenes quietly helping others; being a great listener, nurturing others, always ready to lend a hand, etc. They keep the cycle of goodness going.

The bottom line is honoring what we came to do. If you aren't clear on what you came to do, live your life the best you can and it will unfold.

ANGELS

A re they real? Yes. Do they sometimes intervene and rescue us? Absolutely.

True story...

In the mid 1980's I sat in the Frankfurt Rhein-Mein Airport in West Germany, eagerly waiting for a flight back to the states. With approximately an hour to kill before checking-in to board, I was getting bored with people watching, so to pass the time, I decided to go to the far end of the terminal, and buy some reading material. I would need it, as it was going to be a long flight.

I quickly gathered my purse and carry-on bag, and stood up, when I suddenly noticed a man sitting right next to me. I was puzzled, because he had not been sitting there a moment ago. Also, I wondered, why did he sit in the seat right next to me when almost the entire section was filled with empty seats? He could have sat anywhere.

As I was getting ready to walk off, this strange elderly gentleman - dressed in a black suit, white shirt, with a tie and no luggage or bags that I could see - gestured for me to sit next to him.

Not wanting to appear rude, I reluctantly sat down. He gave me the friendliest smile and then he started talking. And talked. And talked. Nonstop. He babbled on and on, about what, I have no idea. I can't remember one word of this one-sided conversation, but I do know he would not shut up, and he didn't give me a chance to say hardly anything. And its not because I was tuned out, as the reason why I can't remember one word, but I couldn't understand him. He spoke in a language that to this day I am unable to identify. It was incomprehensible as far as I am concerned. Back then I had been exposed to quite a few different countries and cultures, and even if I couldn't understand the language, I was pretty good at identifying it. However with this man, I was at a complete loss. And at one point, I even wondered if he was actually speaking from his mouth.

Inwardly I was getting annoyed, realizing my hour was almost up, and I probably wouldn't get a chance to get any reading material for the plane ride.

Suddenly, the crackling sound of gun fire erupted close by. The Polizei (German Police) were everywhere, armed with machine guns. Something was happening in the exact area I would have been, had this strange man had not otherwise engaged me.

People were running everywhere, it was pure pandemonium. I fought the urge to panic, while the gentleman sat there very calmly during the entire time with a serene smile on his face. I was torn between bailing and not wanting to leave this old man by himself. I secretly wondered if the man wasn't just a little off.

Although my heart was racing, the serene smile on

my new friends face, kind of comforted me. Fortunately, whatever happened was over pretty quick and eventually the announcement of departures resumed.

I learned later that the Polizei were under heightened alert, due to several incidents from a terrorist's group, including a recent car bomb attack at that same airport. Because of this, they were able to squash the attack pretty swiftly.

I heard my flight being called. Thank God!

I had been facing the elderly man, and was getting ready to say goodbye, when all of a sudden he dematerialized in front of my eyes. When I say dematerialized, I mean he disappeared!

I stood in shock for several moments staring at the empty space. As a reflex action, I waved my hand in the exact spot he had been. Nothing but air. The guy never said goodbye, he just vanished! I looked around to see if anyone else had noticed, but it didn't appear that they had.

To this day I believe he was an angel who came to protect me. He kept me out of the path of the terrorists and police. I remember looking in disbelief at the long corridor, where I would have been, that was now roped off, and marked as a crime scene.

I am so sure many of you reading this have your own miraculous stories to tell regarding these beings.

During my NDE my guide showed me a pulsating realm of condensed energy, explaining that it was the Angelic realm. The beings were not in human form, but appeared as a swirling white light. I could make out beings in this light, but again they weren't in human form. The light from this realm was almost blinding in a sense. It was so pure, that I could not view it for long. Not that I was impure, but their existence was in a rarified atmosphere that I was not able to partake of. My guide explained that they can, and do transcend all time, space, dimensions, and existence at will. They can transform into any form, shape or being that is needed. These perfect beings can never fall from grace, because they are direct offshoots of the frequency of love which is always perfect and can never be less than perfection. It would be impossible for them to be anything else.

I did not see that we have guardian angels attached to us specifically, however I did see that our guides can and do request assistance from the angelic realm. Their pleas are answered, and the response is instaneous.

I was also informed that they never incarnate, as their function and purpose is pure service from the spiritual realms. They operate only on the frequency of pure love, which is the frequency of what we interpret as miracles.

AUTISM

After our amazing visit to the other worlds which I describe in the chapter titled *Adventure Out in Space*, my guide returned us to the white realm. At this time we became engaged in what I describe as a teaching session, I, of course, being the student. I learned several valuable lessons during this time, on a variety of subjects, although at the time I must admit, I didn't realize the true value in those lessons.

One of the first, involved a condition we know on earth as Autism. My guide showed me three different souls. They were so beautiful in their soul guises, and glowed with such a brilliant light, it was difficult to see them. They seemed so pure and wise.

Then my guide put up a parallel view, and showed me those same souls, as they existed on earth. Their earthly counterparts were nothing like their souls. They were distant, very difficult to communicate with, and flat out rude human beings at times.

I didn't understand the correlation at first. How could such beautiful souls be so ignorant and insolent?

My guide then revealed to me how those souls had, speaking metaphorically, one foot on the other side and the other on earth. Those same souls were walking a tight rope here on earth, straddling two worlds mentally and emotionally. The veil that typically divides us from the other side, was greatly thinned out for these people.

Back when I had the NDE, there was no term for Autism that I knew of personally, it wasn't widely known nor understood. And, my guide did not refer to these type of people as autistic. So, it wasn't until many years later that I was able to connect the dots, and realize those beautiful souls my guide showed me, were considered Autistic here.

These souls sacrificed their social skills for numerous reasons. The reasons were varied, but one constant remained the same, they chose to exist on earth this way. Whether they were born that way, or eventually became that way due to physical reasons, didn't matter. They wanted the experience of both worlds at the same time. I saw that the degree they chose to inhabit both worlds was their choice. Some chose to come here initially as seemingly normal, to get a grasp on how life is without distraction and then once they'd had enough understanding, set up a situation that would cause them to change.

Sadly, autism has been blamed on numerous causes, for example, vaccines or medicines. However, the truth is that whatever the cause, it was and is completely that soul's choice.

These brilliant, beautiful souls appeared trapped here, but in reality, they are a part of two worlds simultaneously. They are not trapped, but choose to experience the duality of both worlds. As a result, their brains operate on a slightly different frequency than the rest of us, which allows them to traverse the two planes simultaneously. Although outwardly they appear unresponsive, they register every word, gesture and emotion expressed to them. Their spirit is fully aware of all communication and if someone speaks to them from their heart, they will find a way to acknowledge it. But it must be a real and authentic expression, which will resonate with their spirit.

For the person reading this who is autistic, remember you are seeing, viewing and experiencing life in a unique way, that others do not have. This is not a bad or negative thing, as a matter of fact it is a positive one. Your perspective on things is often needed, and necessary at times. You may have a different mechanism of thinking and acting, but there is no right or wrong when viewed through the eyes of spirit. I personally deal with someone who is on the spectrum, and although it can be challenging sometimes, their insight and contribution at times, has benefited me more than I can say. I have learned so much from looking through their eyes, that often times it is humbling how much they were able to teach me.

Persons who are autistic must come to a place where they can accept their method and mode of thinking, only then can they have peace with it. And remember, you chose to express yourself this way in this lifetime for reasons known to you and your soul.

It can be hurtful at times to loved ones interacting with someone who is autistic, but remember they are fully aware of you, your love and relationship to them. It is just that the emotional realm to them does not have the same priority as it does to others.

They manage to absorb all the nuances of life here, while also engaging in a world that is out of our day-to-day reach.

Those with autism are not suffering and they certainly don't deserve our pity. They do, however, deserve our understanding and compassion, and as far as I am concerned, our admiration. I believe they are brave souls who have chosen a life with a stigmatism that few understand.

BEING STUCK

Have you ever felt like you were stuck in a rut? Your life seems set in stone. You aren't progressing, nor are you regressing. During my NDE teaching session, my guide showed me this situation, what it means and what to do about it. At that time, I was young and life was very exciting to me, so I couldn't fully appreciate what I was being shown. But as time went by, I've experienced those stifling moments. The wisdom of what my guide revealed, has helped me tremendously.

Apparently, even though there seems to be no movement outwardly, there are always forces moving behind the scenes. I was shown that sometimes these ruts happen for us to absorb things we've learned. It's a pause, that allows us to settle and regroup. We take in so much stimuli, and go through the motions of life, that we don't always have time to process what is actually happening. This temporary period of null time, can allow those pieces to fall into place.

I was also shown, it can be a time where we get so disgusted by the monotony of our lives that we are forced to take action. We get to a point where we can't stand one more second of the repetition, and make a move we otherwise wouldn't make, which causes a chain reaction of sorts. Next thing you know, we are moving forward. Our attitude changes and things start happening.

My guide advised that during this period, it is best to mentally pause and fully accept the moment of the now. Accept your life as it is at that moment, even if you do not agree with it. Whether the period of time is for reflection, inaction or action, accepting it with the assurance that forces are moving behind the scenes, our lives will eventually catch up. Even though it sounds like such a simple fix, upon reflection I realize it is a wise one. Once we are in an acceptance mode, we align ourselves with the energy patterns of our life, instead of fighting against them. In working with them, we are guided to move the way we should be.

COMPARING YOURSELF TO ANOTHER

(Note: I have copied this entirely from my first book exactly as is, since I don't believe it can be said any better)

How many of us fall into the habit of wishing you had something of someone else's? Or do you find yourself comparing your life to another's and feeling as if you've come up short? Others always seem to have something bigger and better than you: better house, car, relationship... Stop! Making comparisons to others is a grave mistake. We all come on this earth with different agendas, no two persons are alike. That is so true it even applies to identical twins. We are spiritual beings first and foremost who happen to be having a physical experience. Each and every soul is unique.

We have our own unique obligations to work out for our soul's growth, and in life we are given the circumstances needed to fulfill them. That is why one person may have more or less than another, but this not a measurement of our worth and we should not judge ourselves by another's yardstick. Man tends to judge each other by surface attributes, but we are more than our careers, houses, cars and possessions. We are in essence spiritual. Comparing yourself to another limits your own wonderful divine potential.

(Note: that is the end of the copied material)

DEATH DATES

I n my chapter on Incarnating, I explain how we choose our
birth, the people, circumstances, and situations we are born
into. Well, I also learned that we choose our deaths; how and
when we will pass. We choose whether it will be quick, peaceful,
violent, drawn out, or some other way.

Believe it or not, we have choices on when we can pass. We are
typically given certain exit points throughout our lives, when
we can leave. They are what I term death dates. They are certain
milestones in our lives, where we have accomplished some of
the things we came here to do, when we incarnated. It's at those
markers we can choose to leave in the manner of our choosing.
For instance, we may find ourselves critically ill and the choice
is ours whether to stay or pass on. If the will to live is strong
enough, a decision may be made to stay and recover. Others may
choose that time to exit.

You often hear of couples who have been married for a long period of time, passing on within days or weeks of each other. The death of the first spouse, was a marker to exit for the surviving one.

Another situation you hear about, are people who've experienced certain accidents where their survival was considered nothing short of a miracle. It may seem miraculous, however it was either not their time to pass, or they chose to live, despite being given an exit point.

I did see while in the Void, that our deaths are never accidental. The actual circumstance of our passing, is part of the plan. It may come as a result of an accident, however those accidents are planned. Events can be manipulated on the other side and often are by our guides, in agreement with ourselves.

Of course this is set up before we incarnate, so we are not conscious of it here. However, I know of a few situations personally, where a person is given a hint or a feeling that the end is near. My late dear best friend, out of the blue one day, started talking about certain things she wanted me to do, in the event that she passed. She was not ill at the time that I was aware of, and seemed so full of life, so I did not take her requests seriously. On hindsight though, I should have, because shortly afterwards, she unexpectedly passed. Her untimely death was a true shock to myself, her family and friends.

My late daughter in law was in her early thirties, when she started making comments about what she wanted to happen regarding her children in the event of her passing. She was so young, that my husband and I brushed off her remarks, thinking she was just being an overprotective mother. Soon however, she became very ill and passed quickly. Looking back, I admire her bravery for accepting such a foreboding, and still trying to make plans for her children, for a future without her. Although she is deeply missed, we all tried to honor her wishes the best we could.

There is of course the final date and that is fixed. We will not live past that point and its reverse is also true, we will not leave before that point...unless we've chosen to. A paradox for sure.

DE JA VU

I think almost everyone has experienced that timeless moment, where you are reliving the exact same instant over again in your life. It's an eerie feeling, where time completely stops, and you're reliving a point in time that you know you've already experienced, yet there it is again.

Those moments usually came out of the blue, without any warning. Like the time I experienced one when I was simply folding laundry. Shortly after that moment, I had a major operation, and my life changed substantially.

We can also feel a de ja vu moment with people we encounter, not just events. These strangers seem super familiar, despite having never met them before.

I know from my time in the void (*see chapter on The Void*), that there are several reasons for sudden recognition or the looping moments. And we can have several throughout our lifetime.

De ja vu moments can be:

➤ a sign from the other side that you are on the right path
➤ a marker that you've hit sort of an intersection in your life, and it's about to change dramatically
➤ a sign that you and your spirit guide communicated directly for a moment
➤ a wakeup call
➤ a signal of a life changing event
➤ a confirmation that you were meant to have an encounter with someone
➤ an indicator that you've recognized a soul you've been with before in another lifetime, or in the spirit world
➤ a warning to stop, and think about the consequences of actions you're about to take

DIVE IN ON THE
EMOTIONS

It seems like there is an ongoing trend advising people to control their emotions. The market is littered with self-help books on how to master your emotions, control them, not to mention who should and shouldn't display their emotions; men should never cry, women shouldn't show anger, and kids should be perfect robots. And on and on.

During my time in the void, I saw that emotions were one way the soul speaks to us. Emotions come from our soul, and are interpreted through our heart center. The language of the soul can result in a display of goosebumps, a shiver, feelings of anger, excitement, sadness, happiness, joy, etc.

The human psyche has a veil between itself and the soul, so it interprets messages and feelings from the soul in one of the above ways. Trying to control our emotions is futile. The soul cannot be silenced. For that reason, our emotions are never to be ignored or overlooked.

One of the best things we can do to understand what our soul is trying to tell us, is by diving in. When I say dive in, I mean acknowledge the emotion, accept the emotion, and move through the emotion.

Once you acknowledge the emotion with honesty, it becomes less intense. At that point, you are ready to accept the emotion. To accomplish this you must look it square in the eye. It takes courage to do this, however it is worth it, because by accepting it you can see the message it is trying to tell you. Once you understand the message, you can work with it or release it, and eventually move through it. It is not a simple process, and takes courage, but worth it.

The honest expression of emotions is one of the healthiest actions we can take, because the righteousness of truth exists in a purely emotive state. Of course, there are limits to that, as in not hurting another through violence or acting with cruelty.

Constructively expressing the authentic emotion you feel - whether it be anger, hurt or some other - can often help heal a situation that needs to be corrected.

Eventually, the goal is to have neutrality, because only at that point can we view things from a divine perspective. But we can never achieve that state of mind by suppressing our emotions. So dive in.

FORGIVENESS

My husband is one of the most forgiving people I know, and it used to infuriate me. It would annoy me that he would let stuff roll off his back so easily and nonchalantly. I wanted him to return fire for fire, or at the very least, hold a grudge.

And then, I experienced the void (see chapter on *The Void*) and realized I was the moron, and he had it right all along. He wasn't forgiving them per se, as in approving and accepting their actions. He just never let stuff stick. He is by far no fool, and typically won't let a person get him twice. But somehow in his mind, he knows that people are going to screw up and make mistakes, and he has subconsciously calculated those factors, and refuses to let it stain him.

I saw and understood that he wasn't the fool, I was, acting like bitter Betty. When we hold onto grudges, anger, and the

VENIA R

bitterness we experience when someone wrongs us, it creates a stain on our spirit. It weighs us down. I saw my spirit had so many bruises on it, from where I'd allowed actions by others to literally stick to me instead of releasing them. I needed to realize that a lot of what I went through that was hurtful from others, was necessary in order to teach me certain things. And the lesson had to come in a way that I would understand. The flip side of that may also been true, the other person needed to learn a lesson from our interaction. And more importantly, it's also ok and right sometimes to release the person too. Or, deal with them from a distance. As a matter of fact, allowing someone to continue mental and/or physical abuse goes against spiritual law. Send them love, positive thoughts and keep it moving.

Forgiveness doesn't mean giving a green light to someone else's hurtful actions or words. It means moving through that hurt with an objective state of mind and moving past it. When I saw that we set up most of our situations in our lives I was able to look at things an entirely different way. We are the orchestrator of so much of what we experience. Believe it or not we are never victims. It's a tough pill to swallow, but it's so true. There are so many factors involved in what we experience, but karma and life lessons we choose before coming here, play a major role. Also, some things may happen to us to force us onto another life path. Although the initial action by the person appeared cruel, it was the only way to force us to change paths and that person just happened to be the catalyst for that life changing moment.

Sometimes it's a situation where the reason is not obvious initially, as was the case with me when my boss in the military seemed unnecessarily cruel, regarding leave I wanted to take during a Christmas holiday. I was stationed overseas and wanted to fly home so my family could meet their first grandchild, who was born just a few months prior. I even bought tickets ahead of time, assured there would be no problem with me getting the necessary leave. However, when I approached my boss he abruptly changed his mind, and was adamant that I could not take leave. He gave no explanation of why, just a firm NO. I argued with him, then pleaded, and finally begged, all to no avail. Reluctantly, I was forced to cancel my trip. I pouted for a few days, openly displaying my anger towards him, up until the day of the flight. And then heard the news that was broadcast worldwide; Pan Am Flight 103 was shot down by terrorists over Scotland. All crew and passengers were killed. The exact same flight I was booked on, and had been forced to cancel.

That was an extremely sobering moment for me, as you can imagine. Not to mention, I had friends on that plane, stationed with me, and they were gone. I was devastated and deeply humbled. Unknowingly, my boss, through his apparent mean-spiritedness, literally saved my life.

Interestingly, within days after, he approved a new leave request, and I was able to travel home.

We aren't always privy to the reasons behind the actions of some, or why certain things happen to us. Thinking about it though, if we were, it would be like cheating, wouldn't it? If you already knew the answers to a test, what incentive would you have to learn anything?

I don't feel that we can talk about forgiveness without mentioning revenge. I know that when someone does something to us or those we love, the issue of revenge is front and center in our mind. We want that person to get what they deserve, to pay. Believe me, they will. No one escapes anything. It is a universal, inescapable law that all actions must balance. What you put out, definitely returns back in some form. You may not see the effects of karma returning to the person who wronged you immediately, or ever. And it is not necessary to. Rest assured that it will, maybe not in the way you want, but it will in a way that is most effective for them to learn. Seeking revenge only creates a karmic situation for yourself, and keeps a negative cycle rolling.

Forgiving someone is not so much about the other person, but about moving on with an understanding and acceptance of the situation, completely letting it go. It is not always easy to reach that understanding, and acceptance can be a process. But if you can reach that point where you extract a lesson and learn from it, you will not have to repeat it.

HOW DID DYING FEEL

I feel like I owe it to my readers to describe how dying felt. After all, it isn't common knowledge that we are privy to from others, after it happens.

First, let me say that separating from my body was swift and painless.

There was absolutely no loss in consciousness, just the opposite in fact. It was literally like walking from one room in your house into another, except I immediately gained a clarity of mind. I became hyper alert and aware. Stripped of my earthly body and mind, I became pure consciousness, and thus my awareness was magnified tremendously.

I was cognizant of my personality, my subconscious, my spirit, and my soul with all these merged into one consciousness.

Since I wasn't operating from my physical brain nor limited by it,

I could handle the extra awareness.

I did not realize at first I was dead, because I felt so alive and my spirit, so energized. My ethereal spiritual form felt no tiredness, sickness, discomfort, or any of the limitations of the physical body. I felt that I could at any time, drop the ethereal form of myself, and exist as pure consciousness or as an orb of light, which is what I was transformed into throughout some of my NDE.

I did not lose my personality, but it was expanded. In other words, I gained attributes that were positively attracted to the energy I radiated, when I passed. The negative qualities were diluted and transformed into their positive nature. I was close to neutrality, not too bad, not too good. Just my honest self. I typically had a temper back then, (still do to some degree) however, I never felt anything close to that type of anger while on the other side. There was no need to, because I was able to see things from a wider perspective, not just my own, which resulted in a deeper understanding.

I described the concept of space/distance already, but I will elaborate a bit more. There is really no space/distance while in spiritual form because you are connected to everything. You are a part of the spiritual world. Spirit is omnipresent and thus you are too. To put another way, its like being a part of a big ocean, no matter which direction you travel, you are still part of the ocean.

I do not have a fear of dying, because we don't die. We shed this physical costume and resume our existence without it. We don't lose anything, but gain everything.

HOW SPIRIT
SPEAKS TO US

I 'd like to start off by saying that my guide never once spoke to me. All communication was made by what I will call thought transference. It was beyond telepathic, because telepathy is the conveyance of thoughts and words. My guide was able to exchange more than mere words or thoughts, but the feelings and emotions behind them, as well as images, and whatever else that needed to be conveyed. There was complete understanding, comprehension and a clarity that cannot be described. There is no misunderstanding.

In the spiritual realm there are no hidden thoughts. My guide could see my motives, thoughts and feelings as clearly as you are reading this book. I could also comprehend theirs' to some degree, however there were many things that my guide chose not to reveal to me out of what I understood to be divine wisdom, and I did not probe further. In basic terms, due to my level of understanding, certain things were concealed from me. Not in secret, but because I was not ready to receive the information. There appeared to be an unwritten spiritual rule that nothing was forced, and that included information. All part of that divine wisdom.

Those on the other side may use different methods to communicate with us, because here, we are behind a veil. In order to communicate with us, we may receive a gut feeling also known as intuition. That can come from our soul or our guide. A book that we need to read, may be serendipitously placed in our way. Someone may be guided to say something, that triggers an idea. We may be drawn to someone going through a similar situation. We may wake up the same time, several nights in a row. Having a dream may provide understanding about an issue.

Believe it or not, we often seek guidance and help when we sleep. Our spirits travel to the other side during sleep. Often, we will wake up with the solution to a problem that had not occurred to us before, and in many cases wouldn't have.

Another way Spirit speaks to us is using repetitive numbers, like 111, 222, 333, 1111. You may glance at the clock the exact moment it reads duplicating numbers. That is one of the most obvious, hard to miss ways the spiritual realm speaks to us. The number sequence may appear regularly throughout the day. There are different meanings to each set of numbers, however since I have not been shown what they are, I will not speculate on their meaning.

The more we acknowledge these moments, the easier life gets in some ways, and the messages increase. Not that we will never have problems or difficulties, but we don't always have to learn things the hard way. Issues that come up, will be less severe and harsh. Solutions may come almost as soon as the problem occurs.

Messages, warnings, help and love is always available to us. The question is, are we open to receiving them?

INCARNATING

During what I've previously called the learning portion of my NDE, my spirit guide hovered next to me and explained they wanted to show me the process of how souls came to be born. I wasn't sure how to reply, since I had never even thought much about the subject. Then, my guide further explained that I was going to be shown exactly how I came to be born as Venia. Now, that definitely got my attention!

A scene unfolded, and I saw myself in spirit form, before I came here. At the point I was being shown, I had already made the decision that I wanted to leave the spirit world and incarnate. I was pondering several life paths that were open to me. I had so many options, different type of worlds and lifeforms to choose from. Not all were humanoid. There were numerous opportunities for me to choose, however there were some limits, as some of those worlds I was not ready for until I worked on a few things. The choice, however, was mostly mine.

My first thought was, wow! I choose this! That blew my mind. Prior to that, I didn't really understand how I just came to be here and why. I just kind of thought we were born, lived and eventually died. The whole mechanism of life, to me, was one big mystery.

I saw myself narrowing down my options. As a result of examining each path, I decided what I'd wanted to experience next. I finally made the decision to incarnate into another lifetime on earth. Earth was tricky because it was such a dense world, that involved so much negativity. It was tough. Incarnating here was a brave move on my part, however, this was true for all those who choose to come here. It took courage, and we should give ourselves a pat on the back since there are much easier worlds to incarnate on.

Despite all that, I was eager to incarnate. My soul integrity would be challenged by this environment however it appeared that I welcomed this challenge, and this was one of the main reasons I chose to come. Not to mention, I had some character traits that needed working on, not to mention a few karmic obligations to repay to balance out the cosmic scales. Which also involved a specific soul purpose that remains deeply personal.

During this process of me deciding to come here, I saw that there were other souls involved in this process aiding my decision. Their identities were not revealed to me, and it didn't seem important that I knew who they were. However, I understood that they were what I call the movers and shakers who helped pull all the details of my life together, advised me, and made contact with the other souls who I would be interacting with. Not all the spirits who I wanted to be in contact with would be available, as they were fulfilling missions and lifetimes elsewhere, however that was not a concern. We had an infinity to catch up.

I was amazed to discover that there were certain beings assigned to assist in the insertion of a soul into the fetus. Although I was not shown this entire process in detail, these beings were able to align the soul with the light body (our spirit), astral body and physical body. There seemed to be a major function of the pineal gland during this process. It seemed as if so much was connected through that gland.

Amazingly, I saw that I was involved at every stage of my choice to come here on earth. I chose to be a female because this time around being a female would serve me best. I decided on my name, which was chosen because it matched the vibrational energy of my spirit. I saw that the name I chose, was given subconsciously to my mother, through a dream. When I asked her later, my mother confirmed that she dreamt of my name shortly before my birth. I never told her why I asked.

I chose who would be my parents, with their permission of course. This was agreed upon during one of their visits to the spirit realm, while they slept. I also chose to have one sibling.

It is interesting to note that I also saw I'd had a previous incarnation with only one member of my immediate family. The other two were quite new to me, but they were connected to each other, and had been together in other lives. It's complicated, but only to us here. Anyway, it explains why although I love my family dearly, I've only felt a deep bond with one of them. Realizing this, enabled me to resolve some issues in my upbringing.

In picking my parents, I also chose my relatives. Many of whom I have been with before, in different roles. One of my aunts here, had been my mother in another lifetime. A female cousin, was also a brother in another life. One of my male cousins and I had been brothers before. And on and on it went.

It was fascinating to see the different roles we played in each other's lives. Some, who I had felt little connection with, were newbies to me, and I to them, meaning other than being relatives now, we had no previous soul connections. The old saying that blood is thicker than water is not always true. Just because someone is kin, doesn't mean a bond is shared. That could explain why we are drawn to some and not others. The closest bond I share now is with a good friend. We are not related in any way, yet we both acknowledge a deep bond of familiarity. She is obviously part of my soul group; souls who usually incarnate together repeatedly, albeit in different roles. We are sympatico with these souls, and they usually brighten our paths.

I chose the moment of my birth, choosing the astrological sign and planetary configurations I would be born under, that would give a general outline to my personality, and provide me with the mental tools to deal with the life I had chosen. Even some of my physical attributes could be attributed to my astrological configuration, although genes also played its part. And of course since we chose the race to be born to, I could decide my overall look that resonated with my spirit.

In seeing all this, I was truly amazed how involved we were in the decision-making process of our lives. Almost nothing appeared to be random.

I saw that I chose what country to be born into, as well as the state and city of my birth and the neighborhood I would grow up in. I even chose the schools I would attend, who would be my friends early on, and those whom I would eventually let go of. I chose certain events that would happen to me in order to fulfill karmic obligations, and debts I owed, as in the case of the car accident I was involved in, when I was five years old (see chapter on *Karma*). The situations I found myself in, were orchestrated by none other than myself, or actions created by me.

There was free will regarding the happenings in my life, but I also saw that even free will operated within certain parameters that I, and my guides, set up before coming here. For instance, if my destination was California, I could choose (free will) whether I wanted to travel by plane, train or car, but I would eventually get to Cali.

I have at times struggled to remember all this when going through a particularly rough patch in my life, but it helps to remember that we chose it for reasons we may, or may not understand now, but they have a purpose.

One situation in particular comes to mind. I'd had what was supposed to be a simple straightforward operation, that unfortunately turned into 4 corrective surgeries. All that, within the short span of a two-month period. Then, the months of recuperation afterwards. In short, I needed to have several operations, to correct the initial botched operation. After the extensive surgeries, I could hardly walk or move, and was confined to bed for months while I healed.

It was easy to get into a depressed state of mind however I chose not to, accepting the fact that I was not a victim. Although it was a bitter pill to swallow, I had to remember that I orchestrated this, even if initially I didn't understand why.

During this time, I needlepointed, read and caught up on a lot of television shows that I rarely got to watch. These were all activities I loved, and I had a good time, despite my painful recovery.

Eventually it dawned on me one of the reasons I had to go through this - was how I treated people. I am ashamed to admit it, however, I was usually very impatient with the elderly, and displayed little compassion towards the sick. I had no understanding of those who were suffering, or their pain, nor did I care to. Needless to say, my situation after the numerous operations certainly changed that. I now had a different attitude towards those who were physically afflicted, and developed compassion for them. I became very sensitive to those suffering, and saw them in a new light. I learned how to treat the elderly with the patience due them, and understand their limitations. It took this near catastrophe in my life, to force me to change my attitude, but it needed to be done. I truly believe had I changed my ways on my own, I may not have had to go through this. Like I said earlier we will get to the destination one way or another. Some of us choose the easy way, and others the hard way, like I did in learning compassion.

Slowly, but surely, I regained my health and mobility. And eventually, besides some permanent scars, I made a full recovery.

It is important to note that although my guide showed me the process of incarnating, they did not reveal any specifics to me regarding my own life. I received no warnings or predictions regarding anything I had planned. There was a veil in place on what my future held, and my guide didn't even give me a peek.

IS THERE A
JUDGEMENT DAY?

J udgement Day - a term used by several religions in the world, to describe the day when all dead people will come back to life so God can judge them on their behavior while they lived. Sounds pretty harsh and judgmental.

I do not want to step on any religious toes, however, while in the void, I saw there is no judgement day, or at least the term that is meant by some religions. First, when we die - shed this physical vehicle - we awaken to our true self, which is spiritual. So dead people, are effectively still alive, just in their true form.

Second, when we pass, we will evaluate our lives, and have what is termed a life review. During this life review, we will be shown the effects our words and actions have on others, in

MY NEAR DEATH EXPERIENCE

minute detail. The ripple effect of those actions, the positive/ negative effects it has on others, will be laid out. However, the only judging is from ourselves. Not from anyone else. It is solely an individual process, and not done en masse. Love, which comprises the spiritual world, is never judgmental. It is always objective.

Mind you, while in the spiritual realm evaluating your life, you are not of the same mindset while on earth. Your soul will strive for understanding of your actions, complete and total honesty of your actions and accountability. In other words, you will abide by the universal/spiritual law of love and balance. It is important to note that no one is responsible for another's transgressions, it all falls on us. No person can save us, or wipe out our karma.

Also, no one is capable of judging another. We do not know all the factors regarding why a person may act as they do. We do not know their karmic or spiritual history.

What is deemed a sin here, may not register as one in the spirit world. Man made laws are not always in line with universal law. An example of this is how some feel here towards abortion (see chapter titled *Abortion*). Although some here consider abortion a sin, it is not considered one in the spiritual world. Another example of man-made law versus spiritual law, are those who used religion and laws to justify slavery, which goes against universal/spiritual law. Universal/spiritual law is very simple: love of self and others, and acting with that love. Slavery violates that law.

Love never judges or condemns, those are human qualities. Love just keeps loving.

KARMA

I know that many people associate karma with a negative connotation, but there is nothing negative about karma. What was shown to me during my NDE, by my infinitely patient guide, was that all energy must balance. My guide explained to me, if we tip too far forward in one direction, the mechanism of the universe will always try to bring us back to that neutral or null spot. Its called the null spot, because love is perfect balance and harmony.

Love is the bottom line to all existence. It is impartial, has no sense of right or wrong, is exceedingly fair, and exercises no judgement. So, in balancing out everything, we receive exactly what we put out. We may not receive in the exact way we've given, but it will eventually come back to us in some form.

Some may be surprised to hear this, however there is no bad luck. That can be a bitter pill to swallow, especially if we've gone through hard times through seemingly no fault of our own. What is happening is a return to us of our actions and words. The same is true for when great stuff happens. That isn't the universe picking your name out of a hat, and deciding to favor you. It is a culmination of your actions.

A person may ask, why do good things happen to bad people? And justifiably so, because outwardly, situations can seem so unfair. The reason is that, karma isn't just earned or accumulated from this lifetime. Our soul has been around this block many times. We don't always receive the effects of our actions in one lifetime. That soul may have built up some positive energy. The same can be true when bad things happen to good people. Again, it is not the universe deciding that it is going to dump on you or me.

I will give you a real-life example of how this works. When I was five years old, I was in a car with my mother, her sister, and my two cousins. My cousins and I were in the back seat. A taxi driver, driving very fast, recklessly slammed into the back of our car. As I result, I was propelled from the back seat, through the front seat, and smashed through the front windshield. I hit it hard enough to where I cracked it, and suffered a severe cut above my eye. Amazingly, I was the only one hurt in the accident. I had to be rushed to the hospital, where they had to sew up the flap hanging over my eye. To this day I still have the very visible scar, and I always will. Now, I am sure that I was a typical bratty five-year-old, but certainly I had done nothing in my short lifetime to deserve this. During my NDE my guide referred to this incident, and showed me how in one of my previous lifetimes, as a young boy, I had a habit of deliberately, and cruelly hurting others. and rarely had any remorse. Through my reckless actions, I had wounded many children. My actions often left scars, emotionally and physically.

Hearing that was humbling, and disturbing, however it enabled me to understand the process.

Karma is fluid and not always set in stone. We can at any time, through deep remorse and change, nullify the effects of what we term negative karma. However, the remorse must be sincere, and the change real. There is no faking it, because we cannot hide our true intentions from the universe. A complete shift in a persons' mindset can nullify karma. Bottom line - if a person has learned a lesson which has been presented to them, which causes a fundamental change in their thoughts and actions in a positive way, this change can erase karma.

Another factor I was shown was that no one can erase or save us from our karma. And, no one can forgive our karma for us. Sorry folks, the confessional may offer a sense of comfort but it does not in any way erase our karma. It is solely an individual process and only we can atone for ours.

My guide further explained to me, which I found fascinating, was that not all planets have the mechanism of karma. Because we deal in excesses on earth, such as hate, greed and violence, karma was the way to balance out these energies. These excesses do not exist on some other worlds and the cycle of karma is not needed. For earth however, I was told that besides individual karma, there is also race karma, and country/nation karma. I was shown quite a bit about this, some of which is discussed in the chapter *North Korea*.

I will say this, individually and collectively, the old saying about planting good seeds in life is not only wise, but prudent, because they do sprout. Have we planted weeds or flowers?

LGBTQ

My guide, who escorted me throughout my NDE, never appeared to me in a bodily form. Instead, they presented themselves to me as a sphere, an orb of glowing and pulsating light. Even though they were an orb, I was able to sense their essence enough to know that my guide had no sexual orientation. I never sensed a distinctive male, or female energy, but more like a combination of both, and more. Their energy felt androgenous, complete. (Side note - as I write this it occurs to me if those identifying themselves as non-binary here are pulling from their soul memories, since the soul has no male, female distinction.)

During the NDE, I was shown several of my previous lifetimes, having had quite a few incarnations as both male and female and one in particular, which had no such binary classifications. As a result, I came to a complete understanding and acceptance of the LGBTQ community.

Some choose to spend several lifetimes as one sex, and in order to balance things out or experience the other side, so to speak, they will incarnate as the opposite sex in this lifetime. For instance, a person may have spent many lifetimes as a female, yet choose this time around as a male. Although they are physically a male, their spirit is used to the female experience, thus they will display many characteristics of their feminine side. Their inner yearnings and desires are geared for the sex they've been used to.

Another situation is where a person who identifies as bi-sexual, may have a fair balance of gender qualities, experiencing life as both sexes, and have desires for both while here.

I saw scenarios where two people who may have incarnated as the same sex because of their life agendas, were meant to be together and drawn to each other as a couple, despite being the same sex.

Those are just a few examples however there were many such scenarios that were possible. I was shown they were all very natural. And there was absolutely nothing wrong with any of them.

Your soul will always strive for balance, a balance of masculine and feminine qualities. To deny qualities in yourself because it may not be considered socially acceptable, is starving your soul's expression. The freer a person feels to express their true inner self is very healthy, and should be the goal of all of us.

LOVE

"Love is not a relationship with someone, but a way of life with everything" author unknown

The love I experienced on the other side was immensely different from the love here. True love is pure, sublime, harmonious, perfect and believe it or not, devoid of emotion. When I say devoid of emotion, I mean it is above the level of emotions. Emotions are always ebbing and flowing, up and down. Love is a constant force, never waning.

Divine love, which to me is the love I experienced on the other side, is not quite the same as the love we have for each other. Although human love can be great, it doesn't compare to the love that I experienced. Unlike earthly love, true love is not dependent on anything, and it never wanes. It operates in perfect harmony at all times.

I saw that Love was the absolute primaeval level of existence. It is dynamic, and the only power. It is energy, but even more. Anything else that claimed to have power was just an off shoot of love, like of like a drop of water in the ocean.

You can direct that love at another, they will feel it and it helps them. You can perform your chores with love, they become easier. You can send your bills off with love, their burden becomes lighter. You can drive, exercise, read, write, work with love. They all feel better.

Looking at this world we live in it is easy to say that very little love exists here. There seems to be so much evil, hatred, disease and destruction. One of the greatest challenges we face here, is learning how to stay in that zone of love, harmony and peace. But it helps to realize that we never really leave it, we just can't always see it because of our limited human view. Love not only exists, but is the basis for everything, no matter what form it appears, as necessary for our view. Releasing our expectation of how love should be or appear in our life helps.

Love will display itself to us at our level of understanding, and the way in which we need it.

Love doesn't always act in the loving way we think it should. For instance, to desire and work towards peace, love may overwhelm us with the horrors of war. Another example, is someone getting sick, which causes family and friends to rally around them with outpourings of love, they normally would not receive. Alternately, you may have a situation with someone getting sick, receiving no love or care, which causes them to realize the love they withheld from others. Love may disrupt our lives and seemingly destroy it, to put us on another path that is better for us.

What I was shown in the void, was a dot on a piece of paper. That dot represented the source, love. Then I was shown spirals coming out of that dot, representing all kinds of things;

hate, happiness, goodness, evil, confidence, war, kindness, depression, and on and on. I saw that if you traced those spirals back to their source you find love.

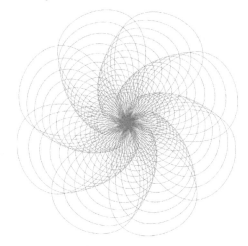

No matter which way you go, the beginning is the love. And so it is with existence. Those spirals indicate all the different ways we venture out from that love, but still the beginning is love and the end point will be love.

Love can literally resolve any issue, problem, disease, accident, situation .... anything. I saw that the only frequency love existed at was perfect harmony. In order to experience that perfect harmony, we have to align and surrender ourselves inwardly to that love. Not to a person, but to love.

Placing yourself in the mental zone of pure love and allowing it into your heart, will literally align any situation perfectly. We can invoke that power in whatever situation we are in, to harmonize it. However, our intention must be pure. There can be no grudge, resentment, greed or any human quality attached to that love. And, there can be no ulterior motive.

When we are in a situation that we just cannot find a solution to, it is best to let it go. It's hard to relinquish that control but I saw that Love is already there always and if we allow it to be, it does its thing perfectly.

ME, AKA THE MASTER THIEF

and the Akashic Records

I had to laugh to myself when starting this chapter, because who in their right mind would brag about being a master thief? But it's important to something that was shown to me during my NDE, as well as something that happened to me while in Italy. Besides, the statute of limitations has run out on my thievery. Ha!

Before my NDE I was becoming a clever thief. My friends and I would go to the nearby mall and plot on what we wanted to steal. Nothing big, petty things, like an item of clothing or a cheap piece of costume jewelry. However, it was becoming a habit, and a bad one at that. Even worse, I was getting quite good at it and had no thoughts of stopping. That, and the fact that I never got caught, convinced me that I was on my way to becoming a master thief.

I was still in the throes of practicing my newfound criminal skills when I had my NDE. The stealing, which had become so commonplace in my life, was something I rarely thought about. So, imagine my utter suprise when my guide indicated they wanted to show me something.

A screen of sorts was put up. I watched as each item I had stolen popped up one by one, from the first item stolen to the last - which had been just a few days prior - until all were in view. To say I was mortified would be an understatement. Not only that, I was stunned to see all the things I had collectively stolen, especially since I had forgotten about most of them. After they all appeared in view, I was shown an equal sign with their combined value displayed = **$145**. I gasped. This was a lot of money back when I was a teenager. The specific amount is extremely important, which I will reveal why in just a bit.

It was never explained to me at that time by my guide specifically why I was being shown this, and of course I dared not question why. I did feel some type of shame though, and went into defense mode, lamely trying to justify my actions with the fact that I had never stolen anything from a person, nor would I. But who cared about an autonomous department store?

Inwardly, I was baffled at how someone or something could even keep track of something like that. Like was there some kind of spirit police unit?

Fortunately, and to my immense relief, there didn't seem to be any judgement directed towards me from my guide. If anything, I sensed a sort of amusement towards my teenage shenanigans.

Fast forward to a few days into my class trip in Italy. A fast-talking, handsome, Italian man slyly approached me out of the blue, and showed me what he claimed was a Rolex watch. The watch was gorgeous, the prettiest watch I'd ever seen. It had, what appeared to be, diamonds and real gold. To my untrained eye, it looked like bling times ten. All I could think of at the time was how much my mother would love it. Unfortunately, although I suspected something wasn't right, I was too young and naïve to spot a hustler back then. So, coupled with the fact that although I didn't know exactly how much Rolex's went for, I knew I couldn't afford one from the store, so if I could afford his watch, I was determined to buy it. I still had most of the spending money my parents, and a relative, had given me.

The Italian and I haggled over the price, and I felt some sense of pride in my negotiating skills. Especially, since at one point he appeared to give up on me because, as he put it in broken English, I was 'robbing him blind'. Heck, I was really good at this. It made me even more determined to secure this great deal, no matter what. Finally, we came to an agreement, I was going to give him almost all the spending money I had - **$145**, exactly. Coincidence? Hardly.

As soon as I bought the watch, I proudly showed it to my friends. Their immediate reaction, however, gave me a knot in my stomach. I had made a huge mistake. They were incredulous that I had been such a fool, and allowed myself to be conned. Rightfully so, they laughed at me.

They were still good friends though, and helped me try and find the shyster. Of course, it was to no avail. He was long gone, with my money, no doubt laughing his ass off too.

To make matters worse, when I tried calling home collect, to ask my parents to wire me more money, (this was way before cell phones had become commonplace), they wouldn't accept the call. Lol.

I didn't put two and two together right away, It took me a while to realize the importance of this experience, and the lesson in it. But my budding career as a master thief ended the day of my NDE.

There was so much more I understood as time went by, besides the fact that stealing is wrong. The universe had extracted the exact amount of everything I stole, to the penny. I came to understand that all our actions are recorded. The universe, karma, whatever you want to call it, keeps a cosmic record of everything we do and say, which I was shown in this instance, in minute detail. I have since learned the term of this cosmic record; it is called the Akashic Records.

The Akashic Records is a cosmic repository of all our actions recorded by our sub conscious. It is like a cosmic (spiritual) DNA trail that is on display for all to view. This I learned while in the void. The Akashic records store all the imprints of our lives, existences and actions of our being. We can view any lifetime we've lived as any species. We can review our soul existence, and what we've done soul wise. For instance, the soul can create almost anything, visit almost anywhere, and exist as anything. We can view those activities in the Hall of the Akashic Records.

We are not limited to reviewing our existence in the Akashic Records, we can view any historic moments on any planets. We can view the lifetimes of others we are curious about.

I was wrong in initially comparing it to a spirit police force, because there is no policing done. Nor is there any judgement attached to what is stored, as there is no judgement in the spiritual world. It is strictly for viewing and learning.

In viewing the Akashic Records, we can learn a lot about the decisions others have made, and why they made them. We can also learn true history without bias. We can discover the nature of existence. All this is especially helpful when researching and planning our own lives. This is an undertaking we all partake of, if we decide to incarnate. It is extremely useful. And as I found out, very accurate.

MEDITATION

L et me start off by saying I am the worlds worse meditator. I always have been. If there is an award for failure at meditating, I would win it hands down.

First, I can rarely sit long enough, or still enough (unless I am sleeping), to calm my thoughts and try to enter that so-called zone of enlightenment. Lord knows I've tried: I've done the chanting, the breathing, the calming music, guided mediation, candles, chimes, group mediation…you name it, I've done it.

Typically, what ends up happening is I can't rein in my thoughts long enough or I get bored, and start dwelling on something to the point where I've totally forgotten I was supposed to be meditating. I've even come out of a few meditation sessions angry. Go figure! To all those who can meditate, I give you mad props.

Fortunately, I've learned that I can experience the good effects from meditation without having to actually meditate. Like cheating, sort of. The secret is doing things you love and enjoy. It could be exercising, gaming, reading a book, gardening, driving, spending time with loved ones, laughing, whatever. Whenever we are engaged in an activity we love, it literally opens our heart center to receive information from the other side. It creates a positive pipeline from the soul.

One of the most profound insights of my life came to me while reading an Agatha Christie murder mystery. I happen to love her novels, the brilliant way she reveals the murderers, always intrigued me. For me it is pure relaxation and enjoyment, and puts me in a receptive state of mind. That state of mind, allows for a direct conduit to our soul.

Doing something we love relaxes us, de-stresses us, and isn't that one of the reasons for meditation? I know that a lot of people claim they have reached an enlightened state of mind during meditation. I don't doubt that, however, it is also worth noting that neither my NDE or OBEs were the result of me meditating.

To all those who do meditate please continue to do so, especially if you love doing it, the benefits are amazing. And to those like me who find it a difficult, keep doing the things you love. The result will be the same.

MONEY

What I am about to say is going to be about as popular as getting stung by a nest of wasps, but I've got to be honest; those who value money over everything else in their lives, will one day find themselves in a situation where money has no real value to them. In whatever way the situation arises, their money will not provide either the love, happiness, satisfaction, solution, or health they seek.

Ever since my NDE I've had very little regard for money. I respect the fact that it is necessary in this world, and definitely makes life easier in some ways. I certainly don't throw it away. However, my attitude towards money was greatly influenced by the fact that I saw it means absolutely nothing on the other side. When I say nothing, I mean it did not exist on the other side. I didn't think about it once while I was there. What I did see, was the intention in how we used and circulated it, which was very important.

Generosity mattered greatly. Those who were cheap didn't realize how they were shortchanging themselves. You see, generosity, when given from the heart never fails to return to us in some way. It's what I call the boomerang effect, whatever you send out will return to you in some form.

That boomerang effect, also works in reverse. When you receive something from someone, and act less than honorably towards them, by either shortchanging them or cheating them. Or, you receive something from another that you should compensate them for, and don't. The universe will somehow extract payment from you in some way; you will end up paying for it in some form. The scales must balance. For instance, a friend of mine performed an act of kindness for someone that was quite costly. Instead of monetary payment, which would have been the right thing to do, she just received a 'thanks' for her efforts. The recipient thought they had gotten over on my friend, by not offering her any money. Despite my protestations, my friend decided not to say anything, and let it go. Soon after, the recipient of her kindness, found themselves with a busted water heater that did quite a bit of damage, and ended up costing them much more than what they should have paid my friend. To make matters worse, the insurance company wouldn't pay for the damage. My friend, on the other hand, received an unexpected promotion at her job, which more than compensated for her generosity. That is a real life example of how things balance out.

Being practical about money is fine, saving something for a rainy day is wise. Hoarding it, with no purpose of dispensing it, is considered wasteful. Greed is an imbalance. As with all imbalances, the scales will tip the other way to balance things out. It's a universal law.

An elderly man I once met in a British hospital, taught me a valuable lesson about money. He'd had a rough life and was dying of terminal lung cancer. His name was Ruper, and he was 89 years old. He lay in the hospital bed knowing he would not have any visitors before he died. The only reason he and I talked, was because I mistakingly entered his room, when trying to visit a friend at the hospital.

Ruper was a pleasant old man with all his wits about him. He was also not ready to die, because he thought he still had so much more to learn, even at his ripe old age. The most important thing he told me though, was that at the end one doesn't think about money or what they've accomplished, but the love in their lives. He said he would trade every dollar he had, just to be told by any one of his six children, who wouldn't even visit him, that they loved him. That was all that mattered to him. The love.

My friend, who I was originally visiting, stayed in the hospital for another week after. I went and visited her again and then looked up Ruper. Sadly, I discovered he'd passed a few days prior. I wasn't able to find out if any of his children had come to visit him before his passing.

I had mixed emotions about him passing, because I knew that he had been in a lot of pain and was very lonely, but I also realized he had learned something so valuable about love. And I knew what was waiting for him on the other side, that love he so desperately desired. He would get that love magnified a million times.

NO ONE IS PERFECT...
ON EARTH ANYWAY

My best friend has a saying that I think is perfect for this chapter - 'Life ain't for punks'
In this reality, it appears that life is chaotic, haphazard and disorderly. It can be troubling, to say the very least. Now, here is the reality - while experiencing the void (see chapter titled *The Void*), I saw that this human existence, on earth, is not supposed to be perfect, nor was it designed that way.

On earth, we are here to experience the snags of a human existence. Its why we incarnate here. Perfection does exist, but not when filtered through human eyes. The energy patterns of this world were purposely meant to stretch our soul muscles, so to speak. It is where we come to work out karma, learn balance and experience living.

It is interesting to me when people get so defensive when you point out something of a critical nature. Although I have been occasionally guilty of this, for the most part I understand that I am not perfect and I am not going to be, not here anyway. Plus, I keep in mind, that my guide told me that perfection was not required of me, or anyone.

Being open to admitting your faults, is not only healthy, but helps you grow. Being unable to admit them, is living a lie. And it's also lying to yourself, because as I've stated elsewhere in this book, we will see all our faults in minute detail on the other side, and there is no hiding from them. It's a shockingly humbling experience, and its best to face those faults here and try to correct them. It's much easier, believe it or not, to correct them on the earth plane. On the other side we see them, but the real test is when faced with circumstances to change them, circumstances which you don't get on the other side. I saw in the void, that those who were at a level of existence where they conquered their so-called demons, did not incarnate here to this imperfect world. They went on to other existences that were less abrasive and more suited to their growth.

I also saw that one of the causes of bipolarism and depression, was due to a person lacking self-reflection and self-honesty. Even the ability to admit they have any faults. That may be a tricky subject, but I must admit it was very interesting and certainly made sense.

Since we all have things to work on, because we exist in such an imperfect world, I find it amazing how others can worship or idolize another human being. Admiration is fine, however worship is misdirected energy. That person is here to work out their soul issues and karma, just like you and I. If they didn't, they wouldn't have come here. Those who placed themselves on a mental pedestal and/or craved worship, had more to work on than you think. During my NDE, as I stated previously, my guide remained incognito and did not require my adulation. Their agenda towards me was purely loving, and love never needs or requires worship.

Back to the issue of perfection. We all need to go easy on ourselves and others. Most people are doing the best they can, given their level of understanding. Being hypercritical of yourself and/or others is flat out nonproductive and cruel, because you are asking something of either yourself or someone else, that is not possible or attainable here.

Embracing this human experience, with all its ups and downs, is such a healthy thing, because not only did you choose to come here, but you agreed to, despite its imperfections.

NORTH KOREA

Ever since hearing stories about its brave escapees, I've held a morbid fascination with the country and people of North Korea. North Korea's brutal dictatorship form of government is known worldwide for its barbaric rulership, cruelty towards its citizens, and its brain-washing propaganda machine.

North Korea's repressive policies keep such strict control over its millions of citizens, that of all the countries in the world, it is considered among the worst when it comes to human rights violations.

The citizens of North Korea are taught to revere and treat their 'dear' leader as God, and any resistance can result in execution. North Korea is also known for forcing its citizens into concentration camps for years, for the slightest infraction. I was incredulous that a place like this could even exist, let alone control millions of people.

Before experiencing the void (*see chapter on The Void*) I'd read dozens of books written by escapees whose dire living conditions led them to brave the most harrowing conditions, in order to escape this repressive regime. The possibility of execution was almost guaranteed, if they were caught trying to escape. I devoured each story of courage, and the incredible will to live that motivated these people to survive the horrific nightmares of their daring escapes. My heart ached for these people, and I was filled with a rage towards their government and leaders.

And then, after experiencing the void, I had a better understanding why a place like North Korea (and a few other similar countries) needed to exist.

What was shown to me about North Korea, was that it served the function of being a prison on earth. In other words, those needing to work out the severest of karma would incarnate into this country. Not all, but many of these people were there because they needed to live a life where they had no freedom, no chance to improve themselves, and no way out. They were incarcerated without being behind bars. When I initially saw this, I was compelled to look deeper. I was so filled with compassion for these poor people, it was hard to imagine anyone willingly choosing this level of cruelty.

As I opened my mind and delved further into that cosmic database, I saw that many were paying back karmic debts from lifetimes of cruelty, savagery, barbarism and other horrific acts they themselves either committed, or allowed to happen. I could see that many had several lifetimes where they had mistreated others, with the same type of cruelty they were now living under.

Issues with idolatry, was another major factor that I saw to be a major reason that many chose to incarnate into this cruel country. Worship of others is considered taboo in the spiritual world, since we all are from the same source. Worship involves a saturated ego for the one who requires it, and does not honor the spark of that source in all. We have seen aspects of this recently in the US, where it has reached almost cult like proportions. These same type of people, in order to free themselves of this type of behavior, may choose a place like North Korea on their next go round, where they are forced into worship, if they do not break free of this form of mental slavery while here.

Whatever the case may be, at some point the karmic scales will need to balance.

Interestingly, although my focus was initially on North Korea, other information came through that was along the same vein, but different. The country of Afghanistan was highlighted to me. There, women were treated worse than 2nd class citizens, and the ravages of war were nonstop. This was another country where karmic debts were paid en masse. Those subjugating woman, like the Taliban, often came right back to that country as a woman to experience firsthand the same horrors they'd inflicted. Interestingly, I saw that the Taliban had no light coming from their teachings or beliefs. And I saw some had no soul connection. There was a lot of darkness among them. They embraced evil, and this shut out the light from within.

There is a lot going on in Afghanistan, it is a place which will make or break a soul, and test its integrity. And it's not only those who are native to this country who have been tested by it as soldiers from all over the world have been tested by this harsh country. Afghanistan definitely served a purpose.

Mind you, I don't want this revelation about the purpose of these type of countries to appear cold and heartless, because despite the horrors these people choose to live through, or experience, they still deserve our compassion and help when it can be provided.

The good thing is, that those who appeared to learn their lesson were the ones who were able to escape, or weren't affected so much by their governments policies. Most of the escapees I've read about, have turned their efforts and attention towards trying to help those from their homeland. Many of them have aided in helping others escape. They've also helped spread the word in their respective countries about what lies beyond its borders, giving some a sense of hope.

Seeing this was a bittersweet pill for me to swallow. Although my heart bleeds for these people living in such harsh conditions, I can also understand how important it is for their souls' growth.

OUR LOVED ONES
ON THE OTHER SIDE

Will we see our loved ones again? HELL YEAH!! We will see every person we want to see, and even those we may not even be aware of while here.

We have an extended group of souls who we will see on the other side. We will see all those whom we have a connection with, whom we love, even our pets. (Side note, sometimes a loved one will insert themselves into our pet to visit with us, while here on earth. Thus, the extreme closeness some feel towards their pet. See chapter on *Pets*.)

We miss the day-to-day contact of our loved ones, yet they are able to see us from the other side. They can feel our words and thoughts.

You can talk to loved ones, they will receive the message. You can tell them whatever you need to. If you have unresolved issues with them, you can express how you feel. They hear and feel it all, because there are no communication barriers on their side. Even if they aren't around you at that moment, your words and feelings stay in your auric field, and can be picked up by loved ones. They are able to read the intentions and true desires of the heart.

The relative or friend that we grieve over here, is on the other side carrying on their existence, and are very happy, as there is no negativity on the other side. They are learning and continuing their soul's growth.

When we sleep we often visit with them. If you've dreamt of a loved one, more often than not, your souls met during your sleep.

For those wondering what happens if a loved one has reincarnated, how will we see them when we pass? The answer is quite simple, the soul never incarnates. The spiritual form of that soul does, however the soul resides always in the spiritual world. Thus their true essence is always available to us and vice versa.

Our loved ones can imprint themselves upon our mind, and if we aren't too wracked with grief, we will get a fleeting impression of them. This is their way of comforting us. If we are too wracked with grief, they may find someone else to communicate thru. Or they may manipulate objects around us.

They can and often do send signs to us, as was the case when my best friend Dee passed. Before her passing, we would sit for hours scratching off bingo lottery tickets. It was our favorite pastime, something we did together, for years. After her passing, I was initially inconsolable, racked with grief.

Then one day I started seeing and hearing the word 'bingo' throughout my day. No matter if I was watching television, driving, at the store, wherever, the word came up several times throughout my day. This happened consistently for about two weeks until it dawned on me my darling Dee was trying to tell me she was ok and happy. My grief vanished, and I was able to move on with the knowledge I would definitely see her again. The bingo references ended after that.

Our loved ones don't always communicate with us, as they are busy carrying on their existence with the knowledge that they will see us again, soon. After all, there is no time on the other side, and an earthly life is but a snap of the fingers on the other side, relatively speaking. Although to us it can seem like an eternity, your loved ones know how brief it is.

PETS

I have never really been a pet person. Other than the occasional fish tank, I haven't owned any other pets. Its not that I don't have an affinity for animals, because I do. I particularly love peacocks, dophins, horses, elephants, birds and whales. I do recognize and appreciate the fact that they are as much a part of creation as humans.

In the void I was shown some information about the animal kingdom that I believe should be shared. The first thing I was made aware of, was the fact that animal souls are different than the human soul, not less than, or greater than, but different.

Although people have many different types of animals as pets, I was given information mostly about dogs and cats.

Cats appeared to operate in between dimensions and realms. They have one paw here and one paw there, so to speak. They are constantly in touch with the other realms of existence and communicate back and forth between those realms. They communicated not by words, but sounds, vibrations and the projection of images combined.

Cats tended to spend more time in the other world, playing and communicating, then they did here. Cats could also communicate with each other over distances, and often did. They also were able to communicate with the deceased.

Dogs, however, operated on a slightly different plane. They are not dimensional communicators like cats, however they have an unfiltered, direct connect to the spiritual animal kingdom. They operate in a realm that is different from the human spectrum, but are very sensitive to this dimension.

Dogs are tuned into the energetic realms. They excel at sensing energy. They are tuned into energy waves that most of us are oblivious too. Think about it, a dog can alert of danger, that we aren't even aware of. A dog can make us aware of a person who may not have our best interests at heart. They are keen at sensing the vibes coming from humans. A dogs instincts and reactions should be trusted.

The most fascinating thing I saw regarding pets, no matter what type of animal it was, was that a soul could insert it's spiritual form into any animal and often did. There were several reasons for a soul to do this. One of the main reasons, was that souls who had relationships with loved ones on earth, could and often did, inhabit the body of a pet to temporarily provide comfort, companionship, love, and to watch over their loved ones. Think about it, have you or someone you've known had a pet that displayed an unusual amount of loyalty and devotion? Have they seemed overprotective towards their owner or super clingy? Or displayed some type of human characteristics? Has there been an unusually close bond? More than likely it is a loved one 'visiting' for a while.

I had an experience once which proved to me this was true. I witnessed a dog's features morph into a human face. It was only for a brief moment, but I caught it. And that dog knew I caught him, and nipped at my feet immediately afterwards as if to warn me not to say a word. Lol. Yes it was very weird, but very real also. The dog was the pet of a friend of mine. I didn't tell my friend, but I was never able to look at that dog the same way again. I noticed that dog had no interest in anyone else but my friend, their owner. They wouldn't acknowledge or interact with my friends spouse or children.

I know that people often wonder will they see their pets on the other side. I saw that not only will they meet up with their pets again, but that there will be instant recognition, because it will be a soul to soul acknowledgement. A soul to soul connection is a bond that cannot be severed. I hope that brings comfort to those who have lost their beloved pets, because it is true.

RELIGION

Before my NDE, I was never able to embrace any religion. The ones I was exposed to, seemed too rigid and complex, especially for something that I sensed intuitively should be very simple.

At one point growing up, my parents sent me to Catholic school. Almost immediately, I was turned off by the rituals and dogma of the Catholic faith. The whole process of worshipping a God, that was supposed to be of love, seemed too pretentious. Now understand this, I am not putting down the Catholic faith, as you will soon see. However, I am saying it did not work for me. After having my NDE, I understand why. There is no religion, dogma, holy books, rituals, or faiths on the other side. Love/God/ Allah/the Source can never be confined in any way, to any one belief system.

What I did see specifically pertaining to religion, was during my visit to the Void (see chapter on *The Void*). While submersed in that all knowing place, I saw that all religions on earth, have some spark of the truth to them. What is the truth? It is Love, period. Man has made it complicated, but that is the bottom line. How that love reveals itself to you and I is forever unfolding, and never set in stone. Love is purity, integrity, ultra-kindness and so much more. Whatever form that manifests in your life, and ongoing existence, is up to your unique individuality.

I saw that there was no right or wrong, religion on earth. All of them serve their purpose because we were all at different levels of understanding. I saw that some humans needed the structure, organization, and guidelines of religion, and that when used to enhance themselves was a beautiful thing. I saw beautiful geometric patterns of loving energy, flowing out from millions of souls who used their religion in this way. Those energetic patterns naturally spread to others in loving ways, and helped them.

On the flip side, I saw that those who were rigid and fundamentalist in their beliefs, and tried to force those beliefs on others, had no energetic pattern of love extending from them, and were stifling the light within them. That light was the soul coming through, and the fundamentalists were snuffing out that light in themselves, and others, who they managed to persuade to follow them. What they were doing was coming from a place of ego, not love, and it benefitted no one.

Churches were not necessarily holy places, but the heart was. It is where our intentions, and love lie. To illustrate this, three different scenarios were unfolded to me. In the first, I saw a mother praying for her son, who was a soldier in a battle zone. Her love reached him. He in turn, was led to silently pray for not only his fellow soldiers, but those of the enemy also. There was a huge light of love extending from his heart center that expanded out. That one simple action had a ripple effect on the others: one soldier overcame a crippling fear of the battlefield;

another soldier lost his desire to kill, unless he absolutely had to; someone else's headache vanished, and they were able to think more clearly; one of the enemies questioned their motive for fighting, and decided to desert. It was fascinating for me to see how love directed outwardly, leap frogged onto others. I learned so much from seeing the effects of how love operates. The soldiers' actions, despite being in the battlefield, were holy.

On the flip side, I saw a woman sitting in church, all dolled up, hoping everyone noticed her. In her eyes, she considered herself holy because she didn't drink, smoke, cuss, or engage in the other sins the so-called heathens did. She looked down on everyone with her self-righteous attitude. Although she regularly attended church, she had absolutely no thought of the weekly message being preached, nor did she care. There was no light coming from her heart.

Next was an atheist who had no personal belief in a god. The atheist was fixing the flat tire of a complete stranger. They naturally spread kindness, love and goodness just because. This person, had more love coming from them, then many who claimed to know God. This was considered holy.

In the spiritual world, there is no praise or recognition given for church attendance, what garb was worn, how much a person tithed, or if a person had accepted a savior. When your soul is laid bare, the only thing that resonates is the love that resides there. That is it. Because love is the frequency of all.

REINCARNATION

Long before I had my NDE at 17, I suffered from severe athletes foot. My feet would swell, ooze with pus, and itch uncontrollably. Walking became a painful nightmare. Although I tried several remedies, nothing seemed to help. The condition would mysteriously vanish for a while, and then return at some point with a vengeance. This happened like clockwork, year after year, up until my twenties.

It was about that time, when I visited a hypnotherapist for the purpose of getting some insight into the NDE I'd had. After explaining the purpose and reason for my visit, the hypnotherapist put me under. She advised me to be open to whatever information came through.

Almost right away, images and information began unfolding in my mind. I didn't get any insights into my NDE, but something delightfully unexpected came through.

I saw myself as an oriental woman, in another lifetime, walking down a cobble stone road. My feet were bound, with pus stains covering the wrap around my feet. My feet were shoved inside some wooden, clog type shoes which only added to the extreme discomfort. I was in horrific, crippling pain. It was the custom, albeit not a wise one, at that time and place where I lived to bind the feet. Each step was torture, and I saw that I endured this condition almost my entire life.

As I explained what I was seeing to the hypnotherapist - who had no idea about my condition with my feet - she instructed me to release the memory and understand that I no longer needed to carry that lifetime, or its effects, with me. I did as I was told.

After that session, I never once experienced athletes' foot again.

I also realized that in seeing this lifetime, helped explain my deep love for all things oriental, whether it be clothing, food, art, etc. that I am naturally drawn to.

Seeing the hypnotherapist spurred me to look further into hypnotherapy, and I eventually discovered the work of Dolores Cannon. She was a hypnotherapist, who specialized in past life regression. Her work in this field spanned almost five decades. I would advise anyone, with more than a passing interest in reincarnation, to read any of her books. She has chronicled thousands of past life regressions, and they are fascinating.

During my NDE, my guide revealed several of my previous lifetimes to me, and I will share them.

The first identity was a black woman in the early 1800's, on earth. In that lifetime I was a slave, and my job was cooking for field hands. Although I had no family and all it seemed like I did was cook, I was a happy woman. I was content to help, and provide for the other slaves, and I cooked for them with love. My guide specifically pointed out my positive attitude during that lifetime, despite the loneliness and drudgery of it.

The next lifetime I was shown, was as a young Scandinavian teen, living in one of the Nordic countries. I was a cruel young man, who often inflicted hurt on others physically and emotionally, and seemed to have a weird fascination with leaving scars on my victims. This lifetime as a young boy was brief - I didn't live beyond my teens. This is the same lifetime I spoke about in the chapter on *Karma*. I have suffered quite a few injuries in this lifetime, more so than the average person and have plenty of scars to show for it. I am pretty sure the lifetime as this young boy, is one of the main the reasons why.

At the time of seeing this, I felt defensive and horrified, shocked that I could be so cruel. My guide, sensing my displeasure, helped me to understand that this does not represent the whole of me. That young man was a tiny sliver of many existences and that believe it or not, it was necessary for me to experience that life. I wasn't given details on why exactly, but I can say that today, I am appalled at cruelty and violence of any kind.

Next, I saw myself as a being who was from an entirely different planet than earth. In this lifetime, I was neither male nor female - I had no identifying gender. It appeared that I was a balanced combination of genders, which was the way of this particular world, with no distinction in sexes. I was very tall, lean and brown skinned. There were several different races on this planet, that mimicked what we have here on earth, but more. There were even some who had a greenish tint to their skin. On earth I would have been considered Black or African American, however I was considered neither on that home world, as race was not an identifier nor an issue. And definitely not a dividing factor, like it is on earth. Class was. There were two different types of classes: the Tech class and the Guardian class. The tech class seemed responsible for keeping the civilization technologically savy, while the guardian class was responsible for everything else. It seemed that my role in this world was to act with others to help bridge the gap between the two classes, who clashed constantly, and sometimes violently. I found this lifetime quite interesting for a few reasons, but mainly because I could see that race issues were nonexistent, which was quite refreshing. Also, that I was a fierce fighter for equality, which mimics how I am today, regarding any form of inequality.

The reader may ask how did I know it was me in those lifetimes, especially since I looked completely different in them. The answer is, I recognized my soul. Admittedly, it is an odd feeling seeing yourself as someone else, like looking at a complete stranger, but knowing it is you. The best way I can describe the familiarity, is that my soul clicked with these entities.

Those who are very racist here will be in for a shock, when they realize that they can and often do come back as those same races they despise. Alternately, reincarnation can explain why there are many people who feel a strong affinity for another race or culture, without understanding why.

Reincarnation makes a lot of sense when you think about it logically. How else can you explain the child prodigy born with an amazing talent. Or, why some people are born with a handicap. It can also explain why some are born into wealth, while others are born poor. All these can be tied to karma. Some come in the form of debts or rewards we are owed. However, not all are debts or rewards. For instance, a person may suffer being born with a handicap in order to help those close to them develop caring and compassion.

In another example, wealth is not an indicator of greatness. Someone born into incredible wealth may have chosen to challenge themselves to see how they will use their money; will they help others or hoard their wealth?

There are infinite variables that apply when we incarnate, and thus no one is capable of judging from this side. We simply cannot see the full picture.

To the question – do all souls reincarnate? The answer is no. Souls choose to experience existence in many different ways and may remain in the spiritual realms, where they have endless opportunities. It is up to that soul, and how it chooses to express itself. I saw that there were many souls that chose to help others from the other side, without actually experiencing the cycle of reincarnation themselves. Some of them serve as guides.

Children often offer a key to the answer of - is reincarnation real? There are numerous stories of children recanting details regarding lives, that they should not be aware of. Upon investigating, those details are proven correct. The explanation for this is that their memories of life before coming here is often still vivid, and hasn't been diluted. Parents should encourage those memories, and help the child expound on them.

Whether one believes in reincarnation or not is definitely a personal decision. For me, I know that it is real and explains so much.

SOUL GROUP

Have you ever met someone

Have you ever met someone for the first time, yet they seem familiar? Or it felt as if you've known them forever? A person who you feel deeply connected to, although you may have just met, or haven't known them long? Well, more than likely you have known them before. Not in this life, but they are probably part of your soul group.

While experiencing the void, I saw that we are all a part of soul group. Your soul group are souls whom you incarnate with over and over with, because they are sympatico to your energetic field, and typically are good for you and vice versa. Your souls' have agreed to incarnate together to help each other out in some way, to provide a sense of family outside of your earthly family, and to ease each other's paths. They may also be catalyst for learning. Whatever the case may be, knowing them feels right.

We may not be related to those souls through intimate family contact here because of other obligations, but we've agreed to meet up in some way throughout our lives.

Often these souls don't necessarily come as lovers, although they can. More often than not they come as friends, coworkers, neighbors and such.

I have had a few in my path, and they have been pure blessings to me. These familiar soul encounters are typically gifts, revealing a shared connection from past lives or bonding in the spirit world. They may not always stay in our lives here, but hint at an existence beyond this one.

SPIRIT GUIDES

Before my NDE, I'd hardly heard of the term, Spirit Guide. During my NDE I did not see any of the prophets, saints or other religious figures, but there was a presence with me throughout. This entity did not once reveal their identity to me, not even a name. Instead, they simply introduced themselves to me as my guide. Although at one point, I did ask for a name, I was told that it was not necessary for me to know it. And that names used in the spiritual spheres, were rarely revealed to those still living in the denser planes. This was stated matter of factly, with no malice or meanness. I did not ask why, although I was curious. Eventually however, I received my answer in the void. Spiritual names involve symbols and energy from the spiritual planes that are very powerful, and should not be used here. They contain information above and beyond this dimension, the 3d world, and this dimension cannot handle it. I can certainly understand why my guide did not reveal that to me at my young age, I was much too immature to understand that, and appreciate that type of power.

I sensed that I knew this person/entity, that there was a familiarity with them. It felt a connection deeper than a blood relation, yet I couldn't place it. Despite that, their energy merged harmoniously with mine, and I knew they were committed to helping me.

As explained by this being, they were my guide, pledged to accompany me during this life, or at least part of it. I was not special though, as I was told; we all have them. We are literally never alone. From the moment of birth, and sometimes before, we are watched over from the other side by a guide, or guides.

In this human realm, the 3rd dimension, existence is very dense, and we often need guidance.

Have you ever felt a mental nudge or a gut feeling when trying to decide on a certain course of action? Our guide is sometimes the whisper of intuition we feel. Has an idea popped into your head seemingly out of nowhere, that you knew you would have never thought of? That is probably your spirit guide.

Our guide may physically intervene, if they see danger in our path, if it is something we don't necessarily need to experience. We may, or may not, be aware of their intervention.

They may provide help, if we ask, and it does not interfere with pre-planned events, or our karma.

Our guide might be the reason for that so called coincidence, as they orchestrate events from the other side.

When trying to work out a problem, they may unfold options to us.

They will not, however, prevent us from experiencing things that are vital to our learning process, or interfere with our overall soul agenda; what we came here to do. Mostly, they are silent back seat passengers during our lives.

Our guides are always with us, and thus we are never ever truly alone. As a matter of fact, I was told, that there are times when we may have several guides attached to different stages in our lives. This was often due to the fact that we may be going through a particularly rough period, where we need the expertise of more than one.

Our spirit guides remain anonymous, in the background of our lives. One of the reasons is because they don't want adoration or worship, nor do they need any. Those are not attributes of the spiritual world.

Our guides have ways of communicating with us. A buzzing in both ears is often an indicator of communication from our guide. As well as what I describe as a brain freeze, where we totally blank out for a few seconds. A de ja vu moment (see chapter on *De Ja Vu*) can indicate communication with them.

Another aspect of our guides I must mention, is that my guide displayed a wonderful sense of humor, that I learned was so natural on the other side. I was conditioned to believe, especially given the Catholic influence I had early on, that spiritual matters were serious and stern. But that is not the case, at all. My guide was warm, happy, loving, at times quite funny, and joked with me. For example, at one point during my NDE, my guide teased me about my hairstyle that I fretted over, admitting that yes, indeed, I should look into styling my hair a little differently. There was a loving warmth and hilarity to this moment between us. Another example of their wonderful sense of humor was in comparing my height in this life - I am barely scraping 5 feet - to my super tall height in another life. My guide jokingly stated that I went from one extreme to another.

Our guides have made a pledge, along with our consent, before we entered this incarnation to assist us. We made a soul contract with them, and they live up to their end, while most of us remain blissfully unaware of their existence.

THE QUIJA BOARD

P lease note: this is NOT an endorsement for the Ouija Board.

During my last tour in the military I became quite anxious about my future. Not only was I separating from the military with no job prospects, I was also raising a toddler, and had recently gotten married. I sought answers through different means, one of them was the ouija board.

A neighbor and I, who I will call Sandra, began a weekly ritual, querying the Ouija board about our futures and whatever else came to mind. Along with my uncertain future, my neighbor had her issues, and was just as eager as I for answers.

We started off every session with a prayer of protection. In the beginning, we received simple yes/no answers to our questions.

However within a short period of time, the board started spelling out more complicated answers. Eventually, an entity identified itself to us, through the board, as Nenth. Gradually, Sandra and I grew comfortable asking Nenth questions, and were pretty satisfied with his answers.

One day, after a few months of regularly contacting Nenth, we felt brave enough to ask him if he would appear before us. The pointer immediately moved to Yes. When we asked him when, he spelled now. Sandra and I were excited and welcomed a visit, or so we thought...

Although we were uncertain how he would appear, we stood up and started looking around for a sign. All of sudden, an orange ball of light appeared in my dining room. It hung mid-air, right above the dining room table. The light started about the size of an orange, and then within seconds, expanded to the size of a watermelon. Simultaneously, it increased in intensity.

We stood there in stunned silence, and then as if on cue, both of us screamed like mad women, and bolted out of the house like frightened rabbits.

After catching our breath outside, we realised, given our identical reactions, that we witnessed the exact same phenomena, at the exact same time. We hadn't imagined it, it was real!

Upon hindsight, once we got over our initial fright, we deeply regretted the way we reacted. Especially since there didn't appear to be anything sinister in the orange light formation. We missed a chance of what could have been an awesome event.

We begged Nenth to reappear to us, several times afterwards, but to no avail. His reaction was always the same, he would spell out on the board that we were not ready.

Sandra and I were never able to convince Nenth to reappear before us, and eventually we both moved on with our lives.

A few things I'd like to add before concluding this chapter, are the predictions Nenth gave me. He said that I would be leaving Florida and moving to another state, which I did shortly after the orange ball incident. He said that I would write several books; this book is the second one I've written. And lastly, that he would be around me for a while. I tried asking him what that meant. Was he one of my guides? I never received an answer.

THE VISIT FROM
MY GUIDE

Many years passed since I'd had my NDE, yet it was always still in the back of my mind. That, and the question of whether I would ever see my guide again. I didn't necessarily want to experience the prospect of dying again as a condition on being able to see my guide, because honestly although I do not fear death at all, I had a healthy urge to live. But always the desire was there to see them again. I yearned to experience my guides' love, warmth and kindness again. I hadn't ever experienced anything like it before my NDE or after.

Little did I know that I would get the chance again.

It resulted from having surgery to correct a deviated septum. The surgery went great and afterwards I was given an antibiotic and pain meds. I was then dispatched from the surgeons office with instructions and prescriptions to fill. My mother, who had chauffered me that day, drove me to the drug store to fill the prescription.

I was standing in line, when all of a sudden I felt myself getting woosy. My vision spiraled down to a pinpoint and I passed out, right in front of the stunned pharmacy technician. Poor guy! What I didn't know at the time, was that I was severely allergic to penicillin, that was given to me before I left the surgeon's office.

Once again, my spirit popped right out of my body, just like it had during my NDE. Except this time, I realized what had happened right away and knew I was in trouble.

Immediately, my spirit zoomed out to the parking lot and went straight to my mother, who was waiting calmly in the car, scribbling in her numbers book, trying to figure out what lottery numbers she was going to play.

I desperately tried to get her attention, but it was to no avail. She was completely oblivious to me, and the fact that her daughter was passed out inside the drug store.

After it dawned on me she was not going to see me, I became a little frantic, and didn't know what to do.

And then something strange happened. Everything froze around me - the traffic on the street, birds flying, people walking, even my mother - all frozen in time. It was eerie.

Before I had time to really dwell on that, to my great surprise, I saw a familiar yellowish orb floating towards me. It was my guide!

I forgot about everything frozen around me and beamed at my guide. In response I received what I can only describe as a spiritual hug. Understand this, when my guide directed love towards me, it filled in the gaps of my entire being. I felt a wonderful feeling of loving energy encasing my spirit. I was filled with joy, but not because my guide gave me that feeling, but because through their embrace I was connected once again to the spiritual realm. Along with this sublime feeling of love, so much information was imparted to me that I am still processing. Streams of understanding reality, and the nature of things flowed through my consciousness. It was like the information and experience of the NDE, that I experienced before were puzzle pieces, that finally clicked into place.

At that moment I had a change of heart and honestly didn't care if it was my time to go, because I remembered the wonderful white realm and the possibility that I would be home again, in that heavenly realm. At that thought, a surge of exhilaration ran through me.

As I was thinking this, my guide laughed, albeit beautifully, as only a spiritual being can do. I asked what was so funny. My guide replied that they hated to disappoint me, but it was NOT my time to go.

My guide then told me to make sure I put ice on the knot on my head from hitting it on the floor, which I thought was strange for them to say. Who cared about the knot, I was out of there!

And then, just like that, I was being shaken by an EMS tech, after having an ammonia pill shoved under my nose. I was back in the drug store, on the floor.

My guide was gone. I groaned loudly, and the techs working on me took that as a good sign. Little did they know, it was from disappointment. I was expecting a repeat, or something similar to what I experienced during my NDE. I could have cried.

By this time my mother was standing by me, shocked to see that the ambulance was there for her daughter, and she looked relieved when she saw that I was conscious.

Fortunately, although I was getting a knot on my head, it didn't appear that I had suffered any additional damage. The EMS personnel, after questioning me, deduced that i'd had an adverse reaction to the penicillin and the pharmacist didn't fill my prescription.

My mother handled the remaining details with me getting the correct medications, while I went and sat in the car, since I refused to be taken to the hospital.

I sulked in the car, because of my very brief visit from guide. When my mother returned to the car, she assumed my sour mood was the result of the fall. I didn't share with her the real reason, because then I'd have to explain my NDE, which I still wasn't ready to do.

At home, I moped around, glad that I had the excuse of having had surgery, as a cover for my sullen attitude.

Later that night after settling down, applying the ice and taking my medications, I reflected back on my guides brief visit. And a sobering thought came to me. Instead of feeling sad at the brevity of the visit, I should be grateful that I had a visit. My guide certainly didn't have to make an appearance at all. Realizing that, I mentally switched gears and was grateful. Not only that, but I reveled in the love that was expressed between us, at seeing each other again. That soothed me. I also became fascinated thinking about how time froze, for that brief period. And I wondered how that happened. Thinking about that occupied my thought until I fell asleep.

When I woke up later, I was no longer upset. I was actually happy and thankful. And I knew my guide knew that too.

THE VOID

I t was during one of my OBE's that I experienced the void. Mind you, before experiencing it, I had never heard of the void. I coined that phrase myself, after I experienced it, because it was the one word that most definitively defined the state of being. Within a few years of experiencing it, I started hearing stories of other people who experienced this state of being, and were also calling it the void. My guess, is because there really is no better word to describe it, as you will see.

I had no preparation, nor warning, that I was getting ready to experience what became such a life changing event. The television was on, which I wasn't really paying attention to. I was lying on the floor, trying to manipulate my limbs into a yoga pose. The pose did the trick, my muscles felt relieved.

I untangled myself and fully lay down. Almost immediately, I heard a brief buzzing in my ear and I was propelled into what I can only describe as a place of utter and complete nothingness.

There was no sound, light, feeling - anything. A state of mind, devoid of any sensory stimulation. I didn't even have a thought, which if you think about it, is strange in itself, since when are our minds ever quiet? I was in a completely receptive state of mind. I just existed.

I was a part of everything and nothing. I was connected to everything that ever was, or ever could be, yet at the same time there was nothing. Sounds contrary I know, but that's what it is. The phrase 'all or nothing' should be changed to 'all and nothing' when describing the void.

The void is a primitive, yet ongoing state of existence. It is a timeless realm. I felt that I had existed in it forever, yet was in a constant state of nowness.

After I don't know how long, I roused myself mentally, which seemed to take a bit of energy because I felt I could have existed in this null state forever. I was not quite alarmed, but I could tell that I was dangerously close to going into panic mode. A tiny voice within me acknowledged that something extraordinary was happening, so I mentally switched gears, and accepted this unfamiliar state of mind completely, with my whole being.

Once I did, it seemed like the whole of the universe opened up to me effortlessly. I was in that state of knowingness again, but the similarity ended there. This zone was different than my NDE, in that with my NDE I would think about something, and the information unfolded to me, or my guide revealed the answer. In this realm, I was immersed in a sea of information. Sort of like an interactive, cosmic knowledge data base. In the void, thinking is not linear, so you are able to see and grasp an almost unlimited amount of information simultaneously and comprehend it, since you are not limited by your human brain. The problem for me arose when I was no longer in that realm, and then tried to process all that I saw, back into a linear train of thought.

Although I am certainly no expert, I have come to believe that the void is sort of an entry zone into another realm. It is a place, where according to what level of understanding we are at, determines what information we are exposed to. I was able to see the stark reality of so many facets of existence, without any bias or slant. So many things that I had formerly wondered about, were answered for me in this realm, without any effort on my part.

Here is some of the information I was exposed to, in no particular order:

➢ There is a geometric pattern to the source that is perfect. Chaos appears when we break from those patterns, but even those deviations eventually merge back into harmonious patterns.

➢ The soul does not abide by nor recognize any religious book, it is only guided by love - the only books available on the other side can be viewed in the Hall of the Akashic Records. There is no book that guides all of creation.

➢ There is no religion on the other side - religion is man made. Many civilizations on other worlds have no religion.

➢ There are no politics on the other side - the spiritual world is apolitical because there are no opposing sides there.

➢ Soldiers on the battlefield do not always incur karma for their actions, especially if there is no bloodlust in their heart

➢ Karma is not only generated for those who perform negative acts against others, but for those supporting them as well. In other words, supporters of Hitler and his heinous acts, would have incurred karma for themselves, despite never having harmed anyone themselves.

➢ Alien beings communicate to other aliens via crop circles: transmitting messages, warnings, instructions, and a whole bunch of information. Crop circles are like the alien version of text messages. They use universal symbols which many species are familiar with.

➢ There is no hierarchy to the importance of life, a gnat is considered just as important and valuable as a human

➢ There is no celebrity status on the other side

➢ Our loved ones who have passed are always aware of us, and can hear our thoughts and words directed at them (see chapter titled *Our loved ones on the other side*)

➢ Reincarnation is not only real, but we reincarnated to different planets and beings (see chapter titled *Reincarnation*)

➢ Many addicts, suffering the ravages of a severe drug addiction, have chosen that life as retribution for dealing drugs or exposing them to others, in a previous life

➢ Always do the right thing by your soul, no matter how difficult, you will thank yourself later. Our actions can be compared to a seed. Seeds eventually sprout.

➢ When a person is in a coma, their spirit has typically departed that body and is taking care of spirit business on the other side; either meeting with loved ones, helping others or a multitude of other activities.

➢ You can pray until you are blue in the face, you can try to invoke the law of attraction, however if something does not serve your highest good or goes against your karma, it will not be granted.

➢ Natural gemstones, are condensed qualities of the divine in 3D form; I call them divine gems.

➢ Humor is divine, and one of the numerous methods of communication in the spiritual world

➢ Many seniors with debilitating mental diseases, have already started visiting the other side regularly, in preparation for their transition - the veil between the two worlds is thinner. In these cases seniors are growing weary to leave this world, which is perfectly natural and designed this way.

➢ The Soul can partition itself in many different ways, and be in several places at once

➢ The Soul can never be controlled - nothing can possess a soul. A person however, can relinquish their spirit to hate and evil, and their human existence can be compromised.

➢ The Soul can assist any method used to heal the physical body. It can also heal without any human method. The soul can heal any condition, including regrowth of limbs because it has mastery over the human realm. But it often chooses not to for learning purposes and/or karmic obligations.

➢ The veil, separating us from actively viewing the spirit

world, is typically thinnest during the first 5 years of life, and also at the very end of our lives

➢ We keep our individuality and consciousness on the other side, yet can merge with the Source. The soul is never destroyed, or diminished.

➢ Consistently gravitating towards the frequency of love in our day to day lives, can erase some karma, and help our lives flow more smoothly

➢ Schizophrenics who have developed hate in their hearts, often have a thinned out veil, that separates us from the spiritual world. This can allow mischievous entities to enter the physical realm and temporarily take them over.

➢ There are highly advanced human entities that dwell on earth, that help keep the balance of energy here. They reside in places of severe isolation here on earth, and are in direct connection with the spiritual world. I saw two of them and their general locations, which I am not at liberty to reveal.

➢ One genuine act of kindness/love from the heart, has a ripple effect and can reverberate around the world

➢ Love was and is the source, the bottom line to everything. Love is neutral, perfect, harmonious, and always balanced, however we may not always view it that way.

➢ Everything is connected: all existence, life, lifeforms, worlds, universes, all spring from one source

➢ Success via the universe (spiritual world) is measured in kindness and love

➤ Those who nurture hate in their hearts will tip the scales of their mental health towards insanity and mental disorders

➤ There are very advanced extraterrestrial beings that watch over not only earth, but other lifeforms on other planets. These beings allow us to exist and live as we will, without intervening, however they will step in to prevent the destruction of this world. (Seen in the void and also revealed by my guide)

➤ There are easier planets and worlds to live on, and there are harsher ones too. Earth is one of many planets where life is harsh, while there are others that are paradise type planets with harmonious existences.

Now, in addition to all that I saw, I must expound on something I experienced while in the void. I had what I would call a dark night of the soul - my spirit was laid bare before me, and I saw myself in my truest form - the good, the bad and the ugly. Let me tell you, it was a truly humbling experience. Nothing is sugar coated, you see all your flaws and attributes with a stark realism that cannot be denied. Understand, I am a drinker, smoker, gambler and I cuss, however none of that mattered in the void. Those weren't considered sins, and unless done in excess they had no effect on my spirit. I did, however, see things about myself that to me appeared to be no big deal here, but were like burning hot coals in the void. Those were actions that either hurt myself or others. I had so many of those issues to work on, that it almost crushed me seeing them.

Those that think they are sweet angels, because they don't indulge in the activities I mentioned above (cussing, drinking, smoking, et al), will be in for a huge surprise. The universe's yardstick is measured in kindness and love. So your intentions and actions are what is important.

You'd be amazed at how every action you do will weigh on you. If you've hurt another, know that the hurt they feel is far less than the pain you will experience because of your actions. If you've been jealous of another, or wished harm on others, you will feel the effects of that deeply. If you've directed hate, or acted spitefully towards someone, that is what is registered. Not your cocktails or your cuss words.

The universe doesn't care if you've spent hundreds of days in church, wear clothing a certain way, or give a large portion of your money to the church. It doesn't care if you've read the Bible, Koran, or any other book from cover to cover. None of that even registers, and does not carry over. Only what is in your heart and your intentions.

Although I did not have a life review, those traits I saw in myself that were hurtful or harmful, and the agony I experienced seeing them, was tremendous. And there is no escaping it. You can't pretend it away or ignore it. It stays with you until you make amends, or change behaviors. When you hurt others in some way, it stays with you. So be careful and mindful of how you treat others.

The flip side was, I was shown some of my more positive traits and surprisingly, there were many. There were qualities I possessed, some I wasn't even aware of, that were in line with universal laws. This was a soothing balm to my spirit.

Seeing myself in this humbling light was perhaps what triggered the end of my visit to the void. I was so overloaded with information, and then to get the equivalent of a spiritual gut punch, was more than I could handle.

Slowly, but definitively, the zone faded away and my senses returned.

I became aware of myself lying on the floor. I grabbed my phone to check the time and realized although I was zoned out for a good chunk of time, it felt like no time had passed. I was still mentally in that now zone.

Initially I could not hear any sounds, and I wondered if the buzzing in my ear had something to do with it. It was a bit disorientating and I had to fight the urge to panic, surely I wasn't going to be deaf, right? Uugh!

The information I saw, was still downloading and I spent probably the next few hours just lying there trying to digest it all. I jotted down some of the key items.

Eventually my hearing returned after a slight popping sound. I honestly have no clue why, but I was immensely relieved.

That brief time in the void, had the effect of fundamentally changing me permanently. I could never be the same. When faced with the absolute truth, it can't help but resonate in a place deep within. I knew that I had the choice to accept it, or deny it; I could gravitate towards love and accept it, or I could damage myself and my spirit, and deny it. I chose the former. The changes were profound and worth it.

Personally speaking, I wonder what type of person I would be had I not experienced the void. I know that I am better for it, and must move forward with the knowledge I gained, and continue to grow from it.

I can't help but marvel at the fact of how what initially was a state of utter nothingness, and could have been a bit frightening, turned out to be one of the most wonderful, enlightening experiences of my life.

VEGANISM

At the time of my experience with the void (see chapter on The Void), I was experimenting with a vegan diet. Physically, I felt pretty good, great as a matter of fact, and could only imagine the wonders it was doing for my body. I wasn't a strict vegan, but had pretty much adopted a plant-based diet, with only an occasional indulgence in seafood. No chicken, beef or pork. I was also practicing yoga daily. So when I experienced the void, it was only natural for me to inquire about being a vegan. I was sure that it was going to show me I was racking up all kinds of cosmic points, by doing my part to save the animals. Not only that, but I was positive I was going to be so much more enlightened and aware.

Boy, was I in for a shock.

In the all-knowing realm of the void, I could see that there are worlds where eating meat is not necessary nor desired, and considered taboo, however earth was not one of them. I saw that some animals were put on this earth specifically for human consumption. I saw that there was a difference in killing for need, versus killing for sport, like hunting. Cruelty towards animals was definitely something we should not partake of, that same cruelty will be returned back to us in some form. It is interesting to note that some American Indian tribes, as well as the Aborigines of Australia, would honor the spirit of animals before killing it by asking for its' permission. For them, the taking of life was sacred and performed with respect to the animals' spirit.

Although a plant-based diet was certainly healthy, and the benefits were tremendous, some physiques are unable to handle a strictly vegan diet.

Regarding the soul, it made no difference whether the human vessel was vegan, or not. The soul can heal the body irrespective of diet. Being vegan also did not prolong the life span, it certainly can make your quality of life better, but has no effect on the longevity of life. We all have a check in and check out date. (see chapter titled *Death Dates*)

A friend of ours who passed, had the worse eating habits I'd ever seen. He survived for years on coffee, alcohol, and whatever he could nibble on. He took no vitamins or herbs, and rarely drank water. He lived like this for many years. Sure, his quality of life was horrific; he could barely stand, was very weak and often short of breath. However, he lived because his soul overrode his poor health and kept him alive, for reasons known only to him.

Certainly, as I said, quality of life is important and for those who enjoy being a vegan, they should continue. For those who do not choose to exist solely on a plant-based diet, that is fine also. The key is moderation with our diet, as well as regular exercise. Caring for our bodies, while enjoying how we care for it, is most important.

Although I wasn't going to win any medals for being a vegan, more importantly I have now adopted a lifestyle that better suits me. I exercise very regularly, eat whatever I feel like, and don't indulge in excesses. I enjoy an occasional drink, and take a few herbs and vitamins. Overall, I am healthy, and enjoy a good quality of life. That should be the goal.

WHY DID EVIL EXIST

I posed this very question to my guide. It was during the time when I was being given information by my guide, in what I refer to as the learning session.

While experiencing the NDE and being in such a beautiful, sublime place, it was hard to imagine evil being real. Yet living on earth for 17 years showed me that it did indeed exist. I was conflicted. It was difficult to reconcile between the pure love of heaven I was experiencing, and the evil that existed on earth.

I didn't quite know what my guides response would be, but it was not quite what I expected.

I was told that all souls are pure, and cannot be polluted, or stained. However, once in physical form, a person can ignore guidance and impulses from their sub conscious, which has a direct link to the soul. In doing so, the sub conscious can shut down, go into hibernation mode, and one can succumb to evil. Although, as my guide explained, many people do bad things while ignoring the impulses from their sub conscious, eventually they come around and land back on the right track. But pure evil was something else, on a whole different level, when a person willfully ignores those impulses, over and over. That is what causes the severe reaction from the sub conscious.

My guide explained that it was a very sad situation when the sub conscious shuts down, and is no longer acting as a buffer zone for the soul. Attempts from the spirit world will be made in order to reach the person, however nothing is ever forced, and eventually that person will be truly on their own. Since there is no love coming from that entity, they will eventually be consumed by their hateful deeds.

We are not always witness to the downfall of these evil souls. Sometimes it seems like they are able to perpetuate their evil ways indefinitely, however that is simply not true. If they do not receive their comeuppance here, they will after the moment of death.

While explaining all this, my guide informed me that there is no hell, however, a person can exist in a hellish condition, of their own creation, while on the other side.

These people will not elevate to the higher spiritual realms, but remain in one of the lower planes of the spirit world, consumed by their evil thoughts and deeds. Their isolation is one of pure agony, not only because they must relive their evil ways and deeds over and over, but also because they will only be able to interact with others of like mind. These wretched souls will not be able to communicate with those in the higher realms, as those realms are not accessible to them. Likewise, they are invisible to those in the higher realms. They will remain in this isolated, miserable state, until they show either some remorse, or a desire for good. Only at that point, does a way open for them to begin to receive help and guidance from the spiritual world and a way out of their self induced misery. As my guide explained all this to me, my thought was how I was going to be a perfect angel from that point forward. There was no way I was gonna be a part of anything to do with evil nor suffer through misery like that. My guide found this humorous, and joked that my becoming angelic was highly unlikely. However, they added, softening the blow, that fortunately I had passed the point in my evolution where it was doubtful I would succumb to evil. And if I did, I was reminded, someone was always watching...wink, wink.

I did appreciate that information, however I became troubled. Even at my young age, I wondered about the people that suffered from the actions of those who were committing those evil deeds. I was extremely bothered at the fact that innocent people could become victims of those who were evil, and posed that question to my guide. The answer I received, again, was not one I expected, but it goes something like this - only those who are in the orbit of receiving that type of negative karma will receive it. Either they were due that type of karma through karmic actions of their own or obligations, and they agreed to suffer through the negativity. However, it was also explained to me that those who did not need to suffer through it, would not be affected by the evil. And in a sense they were allowed to walk away from it. In walking away, it was understood that they could cut ties with that person or situation and not experience any repercussions. Or the effects upon them were negligent. This was applicable on an individual and mass basis. In other words, it did not matter whether those committing the evil deeds were effecting one person or many, as in someone specific, or a country.

My guide then made sure I understood what I was just told. Fortunately, even at my young age, I did somehow. Not only that,

I was strangely comforted by the fact that evil didn't just have the kind of power to effect just anyone, willy nilly.

I knew, because of experiencing the white realm that evil did not exist in the spiritual world and could not. Souls, who indulged in evil while in human form, were unable to carry that negativity into the spiritual world and perpetuate harm onto others.

I have since come to understand that what my guide was telling me, is that there is nothing haphazard about life. All was in perfect order, despite how chaotic and negative it appeared on this human level. I bet if we take a look at what goes on, we can see some order in the chaos.

HOW IT ALL ENDED

My NDE was mind blowing, fantastic, puzzling, and wonderful all at the same time. My guide took me on a tour of other worlds, revealed many things I had not been aware of, and taught me so much.

The very last thing I was shown from my guide was a huge expanse of land. There was a lake on the outskirts of the land that contained the most crystal-clear water imaginable. The water was tranquil, but very alive - you could see little golden darts of light shooting from the water, at the slightest movement.

The land was made up mostly of trees and flowers. There were other spirit souls in this garden, like me. Some presented themselves as orbs, while others were in light bodies. A few of us greeted each other warmly, but otherwise everyone respected each others privacy. They, like me, were entranced with this beautiful garden.

Every flower, tree, and blade of grass was vibrant and pulsating. It was exquisite. The flowers were alive and exuded beauty and love. The grass was like a beautiful carpet of green, that I have yet to see here on earth. Some of the trees stood tall and strong, while others where willowy, delicate and seemed to sway in harmony.

The colors of the flowers were somewhat similar to the colors we have here, but contained so many more along the spectrum, and much more vivid. There was an almost infinite variety of flowers, some I've never seen here on earth, even in the tropics. Something else, was the fact that there was no dying foliage, all of it was alive. Beauty and love oozed from every single blade, petal, leaf, et al.

My guides orb hovered patiently from a distance, pulsing and glowing, while I roamed around the beautiful garden, absorbing its incredible beauty. I felt as if I could literally breathe in the beauty and love from this garden.

I marveled at each and every flower I came across. One in particular stood out to me. It was similar to a rose with what seemed to be a mix of a rose, hibiscus, and a gladiola. Its color appeared to be a combination of red, pink and a shade of purple that I had never seen before. I floated over to it and took in its unusual hue. I saw streams of beautiful lights glistening from it, like it was connected to a cosmic fabric of love, that was pulsating from a divine source. It was not only alive, but exuded a personality. And it was beckoning me.

I studied it intensely. It was about this time, that I noticed a musical tone emanating from the flowers, grass, trees and lake all at once. I heard it, and felt it, ever so faintly. I was not hearing it audibly, but with my spiritual senses which I've explained elsewhere, are a combination of all senses interpreted energetically and vibrationally.

All of the foliage, as well as the water, were moving in sync with these tones, which was similar to the faint chord of musical tones I heard when out in space. The music of the spheres, that exists throughout creation.

As I studied the flower and became cognizant of the incredibly beautiful sounds, the rose and its stems, responded to my attention and began swaying. Before I knew it, I was swaying too. It seemed the most natural thing to do. I didn't have a thought about anyone else seeing me, or thinking that I looked strange. That type of negative energy was not present here.

The rose and I moved in harmony and sync, like a beautiful dance, to the heavenly sounds. More flowers popped up out of its stems in response to our dance and we exchanged a spirited type of love that was exhilarating. It was such a beautiful moment. The flower certainly wasn't human, yet we were completely in tune, like ballerinas. I felt more connected to that flower than my own best friend back on earth.

I could have literally danced with my new best friend forever; I was so enthralled and energised. I can tell you that I remember feeling so full of hope, and was infused with a true sense of beauty from that encounter, that even after concluding our dance, I was marked forever.

I have never forgotten that beautiful experience, nor the heavenly garden, and those who know me, know that every year I faithfully create a garden with an abundance of beautiful flowers. What they don't know, is that it is my way of trying in some way, to replicate what I saw on the other side and bring some of that incredible beauty here.

After I had my fill, my guide gathered me up, and took us back to the white realm. There, a screen of sorts appeared, and I saw my body on the bus, lying exactly as I remembered it.

I wanted to know what would happen now and posed that question to my guide. I was told that I would soon be back in my body. That I would suffer no real side effects from taking the pills, as my heart was going to be looked after and healed of any damage. However, my guide cautioned me about putting my body through that again, as this would be the only time I was protected. I was duly warned, and have never taken pills like that with such utter carelessness since.

I was also glad to hear that, although I would be a bit disorientated at first, I would not forget the things I saw. And that I was never alone, no matter how lonely I might feel.

I took that in, and then a thought occurred to me. Naively, I asked my guide how I was supposed to live my life. My guide replied in such a loving and thoughtful way: be kind above all else; live the best way I could, always choose the high road; that I would make plenty of mistakes, but even those mistakes would eventually merge into what was supposed to be, so not to worry; although I would be tempted several times, never let hate dwell in my heart; to enjoy my life and do the things I love, (this was stressed immensely); things that I considered bad were going to happen, but to deal with them the best way I could; and lastly that perfection was not required of me.

At those final words, my guide then did something similar to what they did when we were with the mer people; they shot a beam of beautiful white light directly into my heart center. I felt the light reach inside every nook and cranny of my spirit. Everything that was just told to me, was now branded into the core of my being. I believe, because of that moment, I never forgot those words, and I never will.

I didn't know whether to say thank you, it didn't seem necessary, and my guide didn't seem like they needed it. Still, I sent a mental thank you anyway, and a burst of gratitude their way. I felt their smile.

Soon after, I felt a swirling motion, and my entire being was pulled into some type of energy field. I was still conscious, but could feel myself being sucked into what felt like a muddy river. There was a shift going on deep in my body on quite a few levels. My ethereal body was repositioning itself back into my physical body. Looking back, I can tell you that it was an easier process being released from my body, than going back into it.

After a few moments of this, I began to feel the motion from riding, so I knew I was fully back in my body. My eyes popped open, but I couldn't see. And then a film came down over my eyes, and restored my sight. I was looking up from my body.

For a brief moment, I heard my heartbeat, and it sounded normal. And then I couldn't hear it anymore. Wew! That was a relief!

My mouth felt so dry, I had to swallow several times just to get enough saliva to open it.

I tried to move my arm, and it didn't seem like it wanted to obey. But I focused hard, and was eventually able to move it slightly. It was a weird feeling, like trying to learn how to feel all over again with a new body. Slowly I began stirring and was eventually able to sit upright.

I was disorientated, as my guide warned. I had no idea what time it was; I had no basis to judge how long I had been on the other side. I felt like I had been gone for such a long time, yet the ride from the airport couldn't have been that long.

I no longer had heightened senses, I was back to the regular five senses. It felt weird looking at things from this perspective now. Compared to what I just saw, everything seemed so muted and watered down. It was like going from a panoramic view, to a monochrome lens.

Judging by my classmate's reaction, they hadn't noticed a thing, which was an immense relief. Eventually we arrived at the hotel, and I was a little shaky getting off the bus.

Part of me was withdrawn. Although I was surrounded by

friends, I felt so alone. I held a big secret that I desperately wanted to share, but couldn't.

I did manage to enjoy the rest of my trip, despite the incident with the Rolex, (see chapter on *Me, aka the master thief*) however I was never the same after that. How could I be?

I was shown things that even I didn't even fully understand at that time, so sharing them with others was out of the question. I saw things that weren't even in fantasy novels back then. Although quite a few of my family members were like minded, and believed in the extraordinary, I felt that even this was too farfetched to share with them.

As time went on though, I realized what I had experienced was truly rare and amazing. I treasured it and was so grateful for the experience.

Despite all the things I was shown, my guide was correct; I still had my share of heartaches, illnesses, disappointments, sadness, failures, and other traumas that come with life on earth.

I felt in no way special, or privileged in having the NDE, especially since some of the things I learned from it, some people are already aware of, without having to experience an NDE.

What the NDE did give me was a better understanding of life, and why I may have had to endure certain situations in this lifetime. Also, I don't indulge in the wastefulness of the blame game, knowing that I chose this life and all that it entails.

Other positive side effects as a result of my NDE have surfaced: I have the ability to dip into the other side almost at will; at times I am able to see the future; I can see things about a person even they may not be aware of; my senses have been heightened; I have very frequent influxes of that love that I experienced on the other side, and I gravitate towards it.

Even with all those wonderful bonuses, what I am most grateful for is knowing there is more to just this life and this existence, and to know that it does all make crazy sense.

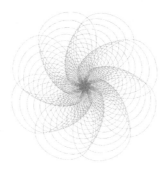

I was born and raised in Philadelphia, Pennsylvania. I spent a decade in the United States Air Force, and have traveled extensively around the world, as well as resided in several foreign countries. My favorite was England! My hobbies include gardening, rebounding (jumping on a mini trampoline), knitting, needlepoint, reading, astrology and watching British crime dramas.

To contact me regarding feedback, and follow up questions, please feel free to contact me at myndefromatoz@gmail.com. I will not however, respond to specific questions or advice regarding personal issues.

Thank you for reading, and it is my sincerest desire that this book has bought something positive your way.

Facebook group: My Near Death Experience From A to Z

YouTube: @myndefromatoz

Love to you all!

Printed in Great Britain
by Amazon

39380768R00089